A TRIBUTE TO
PRIVATE VINCENT CAVALLO

WITH MERRILL'S MARAUDERS
2ND GALAHAD IN BURMA 1944

V. G. Gallagher

A Tribute to Private Vincent Cavallo
With Merrill's Marauders 2nd Galahad in Burma 1944
By: V. G. Gallagher

Visit the author's website which includes additional books, photos, and stories:

VinceGallagherBooks.com

Published by Blue Spruce Publishing Company
2175 Golf Isle Drive, Suite 1024
Melbourne, FL 32935
610-647-8863
info@BlueSprucePublishing.com

ISBN: 978-1-943581-12-2

DEDICATION

This narrative is dedicated to the memory of those brave 407,000 men and women who lost their lives while serving our nation in uniform in World War II. Also, in memory of the families who received the tragic notice informing them their loved one was "Killed in Action." We must remember them and honor them.

"To be ignorant of the lives of the most celebrated men of antiquity is to continue a state of childhood all our days."
Plutarch, Rome 46-120 A.D.

In plain English, *"Those ignorant of their own history will forever remain an infant."*

TABLE of CONTENTS

PROLOGUE

The memories of my first cousin Private Vincent Cavallo's service in World War II lingered in my mind for over sixty years. My boyhood remembrance of those troubled times are still clear to me, and I wished to get these words into print to share with others interested in our nation's history. It is a history that is scarcely taught in our public schools today which, has dimmed the memories of the times when Americans were fighting and dying in battles all over the world. We did not start World War II and never sought remuneration from those we conquered but instead, we rebuilt those nations at our tax payer's expense.

Americans were sacrificed to free the masses from misery and brutal dictatorships. The United States did not win any of the land where our military fought and died. The only reminders the world has are the many thousands of Christian Crosses, Stars of David and Islamic Crescents found in United States military cemeteries located here at home and throughout the world.

I was 12 years old in 1944 when my Aunt Mary and Uncle Fred Cavallo received the dreaded telegram that too many American families received announcing the death in battle of a loved one. The telegram read, "We regret to inform you your son Private Vincent Cavallo, was killed in action in Myitkyina, Burma, serving his country."

This was only months after his departure for duty overseas to an unknown destination. No one in the family had any idea his duty was to serve with a distinguished and secret army unit in one of the most far-flung regions of the world. In 1944, northern Burma was one of the most primitive and isolated areas in Asia.

I remember hearing the conversation at a family gathering when Vincent's Mom, my Aunt Mary held in her hand what was to be the last letter she would receive from her son. Vincent had written this letter when he arrived at an undisclosed destination that was hidden from the recipient by the army censors. I wrote one letter to Vincent using that odd sounding address, 5307th *Composite Unit, Provisional.* I never received a reply, and that address remained in my memory into my adult life.

During one of my routine visits to my local library which was sometime in early 2000, I happened to pick up a book about the war in Asia. I discovered the 5307th Composite Unit Provisional was code-named *"Galahad,"* and it was in fact, *"Merrill's Marauders."* The unit was originally a top secret all-American volunteer combat unit secretly fighting the Japanese behind the enemy's lines in northern Burma. My curiosity was now piqued, and my research began in earnest.

I read a wealth of material including, documents and books about the 5307th and the China, Burma, and India (CBI) Theater of operations in World War II. I reported what I found in print about military leaders in Burma, which was not particularly complimentary to them. Very little was known by Americans back home at that time, about the tragic events happening thousands of miles away on the other side of the world. The words I read were not mine but, the words written by historians and those in the military both, the enlisted men as well as the officers. Those soldiers on the scene and living and witnessing the events. Further disclosed in the volumes of previously secret documents was the strategy, decisions and the outcome of the unit's actions made at that time, the goal of which was to ultimately drive the Japanese out of the British colony of Burma.

The prominent American commanders responsible for the leadership were Lieutenant General Joseph Stilwell and his direct subordinate, Brigadier General Frank Merrill. They were both professional soldiers and patriots dedicated to serving our nation. Each one in his heart loved his country and was a brave military leader. But, both those who are famous and those of us who are humble… are judged by what we actually do and not by what we should have done.

Using the Freedom of Information Act, I sent letters to several military institutions, both army as well as navy, requesting copies of Vincent's army records. This allowed me to chronical a proven time line of Vincent's complete army service.

The research revealed to me information from the day he was drafted at the age of 18 and reported for service and continued to that fatal day when an Army Form 52B was attached to his body. That form showed his name, rank, and serial number, and hastily checked off in pencil, *Killed in line of duty.* This took place during the violent fighting at Myitkyina where Vincent became just another killed in action statistic.

My navy research identified the name and course of the troop ship carrying Vincent and his comrades across two oceans from the East Coast of the United States to Bombay (now Mumbai) India. I found the date and time he left our shores and arrived in Bombay and then was rushed with great haste to the recently captured enemy airbase at Myitkyina, Burma.

He traveled by train from Bombay to somewhere in northern India. Then he climbed into an army air corps troop transport plane or a glider towed by a transport plane and flew directly to the Myitkyina air base and into a raging battle.

I was amazed to find that these details of Vincent's service were totally absent and undocumented in his army records. His parents did not know a single fact about his service. No one in our extended Cavallo family had any information about Vincent's experiences from the day he went overseas to the day his remains were returned and interred in a cemetery in the Bronx. Vincent's service details were buried with his remains.

The medals, awards, and the decorations that he earned never appeared in his army personnel file. No mention at all about his service with F Company 5307th 2nd Galahad force of Merrill's Marauders was shown in his files. This information was totally unknown by anyone in our family. I was determined to correct these omissions as my research continued.

The volume of material overwhelmed me as it seemed I would daily receive another large envelope of my cousin's interesting, although short history. I was fascinated by what was disclosed to me as I read and studied the quantity sent to me by the various army departments and bureaus. Much of this army documentation was once top secret and was now open and available for anyone to read if they were at all interested. I found the information to be revealing and captivating, much like reading a spy thriller or mystery.

Intriguing were the published works by famous as well as little known authors who studied these volumes of our nation's history, then documented and retold this history in their own books for our benefit. Some of this narrative shows a small part of our nation's tragic history showing how the wrong decisions made by those in charge had disastrous results. It confirms how important it is for our leaders both military and civilian, to know and understand the past to avoid making the same mistakes in the future. Unfortunately, history reveals the same mistakes were made too often - time and time again.

Vincent did not survive World War II to tell his own story so, I decided to tell my cousin's story for him. We were after all, first cousins and both of us named in honor of our Grandfather Vincenzo Cavallo, a very fine gentleman.

On Sundays in happier times we both joined all of our Cavallo cousins, aunts, and uncles on those happy days at Grandma's house on 65th Street in Woodside, Queens County, in what I now call, *Old New York City.* This was in the 1930s and 1940s before World War II.

I have kept this narrative as close to history as possible and true to the narratives by others who have written the words of many of the men who served in the 5307th. There are volumes available to read about Merrill's Marauders and some more fascinating than others. There were also several books quite critical about the tragic errors and misjudgments made by some of our most famous military leaders.

It is hoped you will find this narrative to be interesting and informative. It is a tribute to my first cousin, Private Vincent Cavallo, and to the brave men he served with, "Merrill's Marauders," both the 1st and the 2nd Galahad

Force. This chronicle also honors all those brave men and women who are serving in our armed forces today. They have all volunteered and dedicated their lives to serve in uniform for our protection. This must include the active services, the reserves, and the Army and Air National Guard called on short notice and deployed to combat areas worldwide.

V.G. Gallagher 2018

Chapter One

The Family and the Prelude

The World War II years from 1941 to 1945 are still remembered by many Americans. Some seniors from that great generation who actually served in World War II are still alive, and we honor them. A good friend of mine, also a senior who could not remember my calling him the day before, can recall in great detail events about his own army service half a century before in the Vietnam War. He served two tours in Vietnam with a special SOG unit* with a mission similar to the mission of the 5307th in Burma. He is a brave and decorated combat officer with two Purple Hearts. Only mentioned when his wounded leg aches as he ages which, the medics warned him about back in Vietnam when they saved his leg.

** SOG unit: A Studies and Observation unit which conducted covert and unconventional warfare operations prior to and during the Vietnam War.*

I had a very competent eye doctor who checked my eyes annually. He was a very quiet and reserved gentleman with very little to say and quite an introvert. He also had an absent-minded hum that I am sure he did not realize when he adjusted and re-adjusted the complicated lens instrument. All the while asking in between his hums, “Is this better, mmmm? Or is this better, mmmm?”

One day I had a longer wait than usual, and while sitting in his waiting room rummaging through outdated magazines, I noticed an old weathered photograph of a World War II, B-24 Liberator Bomber hanging on the waiting room wall. When I asked him about that photograph his entire countenance brightened up, and there were no more hums as he gleefully told me about his war experiences as a B-24 Navigator in Europe. His eyes brightened along with his face and body motions when he told me about his pilot nursing their battle-damaged B-24 to a safe but bumpy landing after a raid over Germany.

He always smiled at me after that visit as we would chat for a few minutes, two veterans thinking about those long ago adventures in our early lives. It seemed, that he became again that young navigator plotting, checking, and re-checking the position and course from England across the English Channel and then over enemy-occupied territory in France. Then his B-24 proceeded with the squadron onto their target over Germany, the mission being only half over because they must now head back over dangerous enemy territory to their air base in England. His job was to navigate the way back to help get the crew and aircraft safely to their home airfield.

Many of our older veterans with failing memories reawaken again as they remember vividly their military service, the names, the places, and the events. Many veterans claim their military experience during their youth was the most essential time of their lives. These times come back to mind as they reflect about living a full life and sadly remember the faces and some of the names of those who did not return but lost their precious lives, some while only in their teens.

Over 16 million American men and women served in uniform during those trying times of World War II, and those who survived all have their own stories to tell. Almost every American had relatives or a neighbor or at least knew someone who served between 1941 and 1945. This book is an attempt to tell the story of one of the many heroes who did not return to their loved ones and did not survive to tell their own story.

The fighting in World War II took place on most of the seas and oceans and in the skies over much of the world. Land battles were fought, both large and small, in areas throughout the globe. Some battles are well known, and some were fought in unfamiliar places and long forgotten by most Americans. This narrative is about one of those battles in a far off and unknown place in Mytkyina, Burma, and the wartime story of my first cousin and hero, Private Vincent Cavallo. Burma is in Southeast Asia and known today as Myanmar, a very troubled nation in the 21st century and a very dangerous place to be in 1944 for any American soldier.

Vincent Cavallo had a happy childhood growing up in the Bronx, one of the five boroughs of New York City. He lived with his mom and dad and his younger brother Raymond who was in my wedding party when I married my beautiful wife Lee, in 1953 after returning from my own military service in the Korean War.

My childhood memories of Vincent and his family are happy ones and focus on a smiling family. Aunt Mary and Uncle Fred always arrived at our Cavallo grandparents' home on a Sunday with smiles on their faces. I always admired how nicely they dressed and the late model automobile they drove from the Bronx to Woodside in Queens County, New York City. In the 1930s, most families never owned a new automobile. In 1941 my dad was still driving our Model A Ford made in the 1930s.

We were all part of a large New York City Italian-American family with many aunts, uncles, cousins, and *paisanos*. Some may reach other conclusions about a "Large New York City Italian-American family" but, our

Cavallo and Chiara families including my mom's seven brothers, her sister and her aunts, uncles, cousins, nieces, and nephews, were all honest, hard-working, productive men and women toiling for a living. They were the same as most hard-working Americans were at that time in our nation's history. The times I describe were during the Great Depression and prewar years that I remember so well.

Our grandpa, Vincenzo Cavallo, worked as a laborer in construction. During the war, when the draft claimed the younger men, he was employed by the New York City sanitation department. He had to shovel snow, chop the ice from blocking the street drains or do any other job sanitation workers had to do in addition to collecting the city's garbage. This, and any other means to make an honest living by hard work, was acceptable to Grandpa. He always had a smile on his face and a sparkle in his sky blue eyes. I would see him on the streets in Woodside performing these menial tasks, always greeting me with a smile and his shrill one-note whistle we grandchildren all remembered.

We all spent many happy Sundays and most holidays with the family at Grandma's house, a comfortable two-story two-family, well-maintained residence on 65th Street. My grandparents owned their own home just a few blocks from the original Bulova Watch Company building on Woodside Avenue where several members of our family worked.

Warmly remembered are the many Cavallo family picnics and outings when the clan would assemble at Grandma's house early on a Sunday morning after mass. Several cars were loaded up with cousins, aunts and uncles, food and beverage. We would travel in convoy-like style to Sunken Meadow, Alley Pond Park, Lloyds Neck Beach, Jones Beach, Rockaway Beach, and other recreational destinations on Long Island's many parks and beaches.

Our family was represented by aunts and uncles not only Italian but Polish, Lithuanian, German, and Irish, which of course, included my mom's hubby an Irishman, John Aloysius Gallagher from Scranton, Pennsylvania. These memories remain fresh in my mind and were the happy times before the advent of World War II.

In the 1930s the Cavallo, Chiara, and Gallagher cousins all grew up in three of the five New York City boroughs - Queens, Bronx, and Manhattan. This was in the pit of the Great Depression but, we all enjoyed warm, cozy, and loving homes with plenty to eat, much of it grown in our own gardens. My dad and my grandfather, Vincenzo Cavallo planted an extra-large Victory garden in the empty lot behind our garage. During the war years, all Americans were encouraged to plant Victory gardens on any plot of ground available to the population. We enjoyed the vegetables and the peach trees we nurtured. Every Italian family I knew had a fig tree and grapes growing on an arbor someplace on their property.

The Gallagher household in Woodside also enjoyed fresh eggs every morning from our chicken coup. Food rationing was discussed by our parents but was not something we cousins ever talked about. What was more important to our generation was the gasoline rationing that prevented many of our

Sunday excursions until my dad closed his plumbing business and took a job at the Port Kearney, New Jersey, ship building yard. There, he worked as a high paid steamfitter making destroyer escorts, a smaller, very popular warship. Many hundreds if not thousands were made for convoy protection throughout the war years. As a critical war worker who needed gas to carpool fellow workers to and from war work, he received a more generous gas ration card.

In the early days of the 1940s, during World War II, the population of New York City felt the anxieties of war as more and more family and friends were called to serve. The most frightening memory was the sound in the middle of the night of the eerie wail of air raid sirens announcing air alerts. The neighborhood air raid wardens are also remembered wearing white helmets and carrying gas masks. They scrambled about the area with flashlights, scolding everyone to "Douse those lights."

Thankfully for America, bombs never fell on any of our 48 states during the war, although armed balloons were launched in

Japan and sent across the Pacific Ocean and caught by the prevailing winds to be carried all the way on to the northwestern states of Washington and Oregon. Many exploded when landing and caused wildfires, which was the enemy's intent.

The Pacific Northwest forests were part of our nation's resource for the important lumber. This was needed to crate all the war materials and, the smart Japanese knew this because they had surveilled our country for many years.

As a matter of fact many nations, friend and foe alike, had informants living openly in the United States. They watched us closely and reported any intelligence they could discover that would benefit their own nation. The USA was an open and free nation, so it was quite easy for anyone interested to gather this information. The Japanese were among the many nations who were expert in espionage.

It took the surprise attack on Pearl Harbor on December 7th, 1941, to awaken our nation's leaders to the fact that we knew nothing at all about our enemy's intent. Once

President Franklin Roosevelt realized this weakness of ours, he recruited and instructed William J. "Wild Bill" Donovan to form a worldwide intelligence network named the Office of Strategic Services (OSS). Donovan was a World War I hero and officer who earned our nation's highest military honor for heroism, "The Congressional Medal of Honor." He served with the famed "Fighting 69th, a New York City National Guard unit fighting in France.

In the 1940s Donovan was a successful New York City attorney and also a notable Republican. Democrat Roosevelt wanted a bipartisan mix among our leadership and gave Donovan this important role. "Wild Bill" served his Commander-in-Chief honorably and was so successful the OSS grew to become the world's most significant intelligence gathering organization. Today it is known throughout the world as the Central Intelligence Agency (CIA).

Our leaders in Washington, D.C., did not know at the beginning of the war that the Japanese had developed and were then actually manufacturing super-sized submarines capable of carrying an attack aircraft. The plan for the pilot and the plane would be a one way mission. The enemy secret strategy was to use these weapons to cripple our nation by attacking and destroying the locks of the Panama Canal, which fortunately never happened.

The Canal enabled our navy to quickly move warships between the Atlantic and the Pacific Oceans. Otherwise we had to send our warships many miles all the way around the southernmost tip of South America. Then, to travel north up the west coast of the friendly Latin American continent to join our fleet in the far reaches of the Pacific Ocean. The canal saved vital time for our warships to join our Pacific fleet headquartering in the Hawaiian Islands which, reduced the trip by many weeks.

The Panama Canal was critical to our national defense and had to be protected at all costs. A sudden air strike coming from these unknown underwater craft could have brought a quick victory to Japan in those early days of the war. The Japanese were counting on sudden secret attacks to catch the USA totally unprepared for naval warfare in the Pacific. After the attack on Pearl Harbor and the advent of war in the Pacific, it was a poor time for the U.S. Navy to finally listen to and act on the complaints of our seaman about our defective torpedoes. For years the navy protested to Washington about this problem. Our torpedoes did not explode when hitting the targets, and some went astray in all directions except at the enemy. It took over a year to remedy this tragic neglect by our nation's leaders.

The navy's proficiency in aerial dive bombing both, for the brave pilots and the Douglas Dauntless dive bomber aircraft they were flying, assured our victory at the Battle of Midway. During the battle not one of our torpedo's exploded on an enemy ship. All flights of the outdated torpedo bomber the Douglas TBD Devastator aircraft with a crew of three, were destroyed by the Japanese during the battle. That torpedo bombing failure experience proved to the navy's top brass the torpedoes were defective. All Devastator aircraft were quickly withdrawn from combat operations. The dive bombers saved the day at that historic turning point in the Pacific war.

Americans at home in the Eastern states did not realize at the time how close the war could have come to us. Hidden from the allies, the Germans had already developed a long-range bomber under the guise of a luxury airliner. This was the four-engine Condor made for the German commercial airline company *Lufthansa* but used instead by *The Luftwaffe* (German Air Force). The Condor flew over the Atlantic Ocean to attack allied shipping delivering important food and wartime supplies to Europe and also to alert the German submarines to find the allied convoys. Germany was developing long-range bomber technology to hopefully extend the range to bomb New York City and Washington, DC. Although the German aircraft designers, scientists, and industrialists tried, they did not perfect a long-range bomber in time to use against our American homeland.

The Germans also were closer than we knew about to nuclear and long-range missile development. Thank God, the war came to an end before Germany developed nuclear weapons of mass destruction. One main reason this did not happen was the secret British and Norwegian commando assault on a heavy water manufacturing plant on an isolated hilltop in Norway. Without this essential element, it set back the German nuclear research by many years.

However, the Germans were well advanced and deployed aggressive missile technology against London and its suburbs. This killed and terrorized many thousands of civilians throughout the war. The German Messerschmitt 262 twin engine jet aircraft surprised the Allies when they appeared in the last ditch effort by Germany in the closing months of the war in Europe.

The second nation belonging to the three main Axis enemies was Imperialist Italy led by the fascist dictator, Benito Mussolini. Although Italy was still a monarchy, King Emmanuel III was only a figurehead ruler. He was fated to be the last monarch of the House of Savoy royal family when Italy became a republic in 1946. Italy was an aviation pioneer since the 1920s when they sent an air fleet of 24 seaplanes from Italy across the Atlantic Ocean to Chicago before the war in the 1930s. Italo Balbo led this flight when he was in charge of the Italian Royal Air Force and Italy received international acclaim for this achievement. The Italians were in the advanced stages of developing long-range bombers when they surrendered to the Allies in 1943.

The sneak attack by Imperial Japanese Naval air forces on Pearl Harbor on December 7th, 1941, started the war between our two nations. This attack caught our military forces totally surprised and unprepared for a war in the Pacific. The first six months of 1942 proved the Japanese were ready and able to rapidly advance throughout the western Pacific and Southeast Asia and seemed at the time to be unbeatable.

We suffered the largest defeat in our nation's history when 76,000 American and Filipino forces surrendered to the Japanese in the Philippine Islands in April 1942. Only one month later, an additional 13,000 Americans surrendered on the Island of Corregidor in

Manila Bay. This defeat caused thousands of American and allied civilians and families to be captured and then to face and endure a dreadful three years in brutal captivity. The Japanese mistreated there prisoners arrogantly and inhumanely both the military and civilian as well.

Early 1942 was indeed bleak for our nation, and our leaders in Washington, D.C. were hoping for and desperately needed some kind of a victory for our forces. While, the Japanese continued their unstopped conquest of coastal China, Southeast Asia and the Southwestern Pacific. The Japanese aggression was now threatening and closing in on our ally, Australia.

In April 1942, we retaliated with a surprise air attack on the Japanese home islands that, their Prime Minister General Hideki Tojo, had promised would and could not ever happen. Sixteen B-25 Mitchell Medium Bombers secretly bombed Japan when Colonel Jimmy Doolittle led bombers flying off the aircraft carrier, Hornet. The carrier steamed to within striking distance of the

Western Pacific approaches to Japan. All the world took notice and wondered where the airplanes came from. The entire world thought bombers were too big to fly off aircraft carriers.

It was a gallant gesture but little practical military damage was actually done. Fifteen planes survived the raid, but short on fuel, crashed in China. One plane landed safely in Vladivostok, Russia only to be interned because Russia was not at war with Japan in 1942. All 80 crew members survived the raid, however, eight were captured and three were executed by Japanese troops in China. The brutal enemy continued committing horrible atrocities against captured military and civilians until the defeat of Japan after the atomic bomb strikes on Hiroshima and Nagasaki.

The attack led by Jimmy Doolittle was the first good news we could report on the Pacific war. Soon after, the tables were turned when the U.S. Navy defeated the Imperial Japanese Navy at the defining Battle of Midway in June 1942. A credit to the craftiness of our own navy intelligence personnel and, the combined prowess of our navy dive bombing expertise and aircraft technology assured this victory.

Our force of three carriers met the enemy's four carriers, resulting in a stunning Japanese loss of four carriers to one of our own carriers the Yorktown. This reversed roles with the U.S. Navy now on the offensive to last for the remaining years of the war in the Pacific.

We were now becoming the experts in the art of the war's most important weapon enemy intelligence. When, the U.S. Navy broke the Imperial Japanese Naval Code. The reason we knew the Japanese attack force of four aircraft carriers was heading for Midway Island is because U.S. Navy eavesdroppers to Japanese radio transmissions repeated a code number that a creative navy radioman reported. The radio transmitters on Midway Island falsely reported that the water distillation system had broken down, and they were running out of drinking water. The Japanese listening to our transmissions forwarded on to

Tokyo that code number was short of drinking water.

The cat was now out of the bag, and we knew the enemy target was to be Midway Island a very important airbase, refueling and provisioning location. And, the U.S. Navy was waiting ready to pounce.

During those terrible early days of the war, we in New York City were concerned about the German submarine attacks close to our harbor and all along the expanse of our East Coast. The Cavallo family was concerned about our Uncle Jack Toland, a Chief Steward with an officer's rating in the Merchant Marine. These sailors were civilians and a much forgotten force of brave men risking their lives every day on the dangerous sea lanes throughout the world. Uncle Jack served on oil tankers sailing from Port Arthur, Texas, and New Orleans, Louisiana, and up the East Coast, which kept him in constant danger. The ships then assembled in convoys for the long and perilous voyage across the Atlantic Ocean to England. We shared this worry with our Aunt Lucy Cavalla, Jack's wife.

The concern grew as more and more of our family members and neighbors followed the hazardous path into harm's way as the war progressed. The American battle casualties of killed and wounded in action increased, which also drastically increased the "We regret to inform you," telegrams sent to the next of kin.

We at home attended demonstrations showing how to pour sand on incendiary bombs. I recall accompanying my mother when she was taking a course on first aid with many other Woodside women volunteers. As a multi-family home owner (more than two families) my dad, with his two sons to help, had to place buckets of sand and a shovel on the second floor of our home. This was next to the entrances of the two apartments we rented. Our thoughts and prayers were for all our brothers, uncles, cousins, and neighbors who left to serve in the military. There were seventeen close relatives on both the Gallagher and the Cavallo/Chiara side of my family who served in uniform during the war.

Our home street on 59th in Woodside began on Broadway and ran through 37th, 38th, and 39th Avenues and was only three blocks long. Within that small area there were mostly small single-family or two-family homes, several empty lots, and one three-story apartment building. But there were over twenty-five young men and one older officer that I can recall serving in the armed forces, maybe even more that I have forgotten about. The point is, military uniforms crowded out civilian clothing in all the congested areas throughout New York City during World War II.

Between the age of 9 and 13, I corresponded with many relatives in the service. My older brother Michael John served in the navy for a brief period until an unwanted medical discharge forced him back to the safety of our home. I recall all the melancholy farewell parties for our loved ones and our friends and neighbors when they sent their young men off to face the unknown.

Chapter Two

Vincent Answers the Call

Well remembered was the farewell party for my Cousin Vincent held at my grandparent's home. Everyone was saying goodbye to him and wishing him good luck. Each one of Vincent's uncles, including my dad, shook his hand. That hand clasp contained the few dollars everyone gave him, along with some sage advice thought to be helpful. This was the custom for all those sad farewells. For the Cavallo family at that party, that was the very last time we would ever see Vincent.

At the age of 18, Vincent answered the draft call on February 27th, 1943, and reported for induction into the army. He received his indoctrination at Camp Upton, located in Yaphank, Long Island. It was at Camp Upton when new recruit now, Private Vincent Cavallo, received his first initiation into his new life as a soldier. This began first with standing in a long line to receive his issue of GI clothing, and I am sure he was surprised by how fast this was all happening.

Next, he waited in another long line, this time to receive his many immunization shots. As a new recruit he must have heard the stories from the guys before him who warned about the dreadful six-inch-long needles the medics used to give all those mysterious sounding immunization injections.

Back in 1943, many inductees never had an injection that they could even remember. So, there was a natural fear of the unknown for the recruits and an opportunity for the more senior GIs to have some fun. I know because I experienced the same razzing when I got my first immunization shots in 1947 when I joined the National Guard but, that's another story.

Some recruits were so terrified about receiving these shots that when their own turn came, they closed their eyes and didn't even notice the tiny pinprick when the medic actually stuck the needle in their arm. This made them even more determined to terrorize the new guys. It was all just part of becoming a soldier.

Vincent's immunization record known as a "Shot Card" to the troops, show that he received quite a few more additional shots during training and again before being sent overseas. After those first days of army life at Camp Upton and the great speed at which it was occurring, he was quickly marched off to a troop train and sent by rail to Camp Swift, Texas, located near Austin. On March 6th, 1943, he reported to A Company 303rd Infantry Regiment, 97th Infantry Division to train as a rifleman. The newly formed 97th Division was training for combat in the Asiatic/Pacific Theater of Operations.

The training at Camp Swift was very intense and challenging to the new recruits as well as the more experienced troops. After months of training, first in the cold and rainy weather, then in the heat of central Texas, PVT Cavallo was fast becoming a hardened infantryman. His personnel record reveals his high marks for "Character - Excellent" and "Efficiency as a Soldier - Excellent."

When Phase One of training was completed, he was rewarded with a furlough in

July 1943. The photo many in the family had and appears on the cover of this book show Vincent in uniform. It also shows him wearing the patch of the 97th Infantry Division, a white trident on a blue shield. My mom was Vincent's Aunt Nellie Donatella Cavallo Gallagher, who placed this picture in our dining room, and there it remained for many years next to the picture of my older brother, Michael John, in his navy uniform. Vincent's nephew and namesake, Vincent Cavallo, sent me a photo of his Grandmother Mary and his Uncle Vincent, which was taken during that last furlough. In the photo Mom and son looked very joyful, both with the happy smiles I remembered as a child.

During his furlough, Vincent enjoyed all the comforts of home, including his mom's cooking. He enjoyed what was to be his last time of fun with his hometown friends in the Bronx. He probably went to see Grandma and Grandpa Cavallo in Queens. He no doubt enjoyed his Grandma's famous homemade ravioli that she always prepared for special occasions like her Grandson Vincent's visit to her home now, dressed in a soldier's uniform.

For those who remember those ravioli, and for those who never had the pleasure, they were the best ravioli in the entire "World of Ravioli." She made her own pasta, cut up in squares and stuffed with a mixture of ricotta cheese, parsley, seasoning known only to her, and added of course, the most important ingredient…love! God bless all those Italian and other "Old World" grandmas. How they must have worried and prayed every day for their grandsons who were away from home fighting and serving in places throughout the world with names the Grandma's could not even pronounce.

Upon Private Cavallo's return to Camp Swift, the 97th Division entered Phase Two of several more months of advanced infantry training. This move was to further condition and prepare all the division for the challenging maneuvers in the swamps, bayous, and back country of Louisiana, scheduled for the fall and winter 1943-44.

In October 1943 Vincent once again boarded a troop train and was sent with his unit to Camp Polk, Louisiana, to participate in the maneuvers. These events kept the division in the field for over three months as each unit of the division had its turn living in the field and sleeping in pup tents.

Considerable planning went into the preparation for these exercises, and even after receiving favorable weather reports provided by the army meteorologists, the unexpected happened. Louisiana was hit with heavy rains and had one of the coldest winters ever recorded. The 97th Division historian wrote,

"The rain, sleet and snow turned roads into quagmires. Christmas 1943 was spent under leaden December skies and long remembered by the troops." To a field soldier, rain and cold meant only one thing, misery.

The troops shared their pup tents, each soldier had one half the tent, thus the term "shelter half." A buddy had the other half which when buttoned up together, made up one tent to shelter two men. In addition to a shelter half, each man was issued either a rain poncho or a rain coat. One or the other was placed on the ground to become their "bed." Each man had their own 2 woolen GI blankets for warmth. No inflatable air mattresses or snug sleeping bags to help make the troops life a little more comfortable were available in those bygone days of soldiering. These luxuries would have to wait for a future generation of U.S. soldiers.

With their entrenching tools, they dug a trench a few inches deep around the perimeter of the tent to divert the rain water away from their tent sometimes, only diverting the water to drain into someone else's tent who in turn did the same. This was the life they were being trained to live as U.S. Army Infantrymen in the 1940s.

The two-man tent became the sleeping quarters for as long as you stayed in one location. In combat, armies are usually on the move, so in training they were moved about several times. In addition to breaking down the tent and setting it up again at another location, day or night, rain or shine, each new encampment also meant digging a new foxhole. The two man "buddy system" was in use and one GI was issued a small folding shovel and his buddy was issued a small take-down pick mattock enabling them to dig their shared foxhole.

Some of the meals provided were probably either C or K rations. The C ration was not bad with some variety, fairly tasty with plenty of salt, and they had some bulk to fill you up. The entrées came with some variety in a 10 ounce can called a meat unit, which could be franks and beans or meat and spaghetti, chicken and vegetables, ham and lima beans, pork or chicken and rice, or several other combinations. This gave the GIs an opportunity to swap and trade.

Another can, called the bread unit, contained two round hard biscuits, compressed cereal, peanuts or raisins, powdered sugar, coffee, lemon, orange, or cocoa, and a small can of jam. An accessory pack included a pack of four popular, and in some rations, an unknown brand of cigarettes, matches, chewing gum, water purification tablets, toilet tissue, and an ingenious device called the "GI can opener."

This was a small folding device that when unfolded could easily open any sized can. A convenient hole was stamped on one end so folded they could simply be hung on the soldier's dog tag chain where many GIs kept them. A somewhat larger copy of the GI can opener can still be found today at camping goods stores.

The K ration was something else. Picture a box 12 inches long by three inches wide by 1 inch thick, about the size of the then popular "Cracker Jack" snack box. The K rations contained a little round shoe polish sized can of chopped ham and egg or veal loaf or a processed cheese something as a main course, a D ration bar, a fruit bar, 2 hard, round biscuits, chewing gum, sugar packet, salt tablets, Halazone water purification tablets, and 4 cigarettes and matches. K ration came in three varieties: breakfast, lunch, and supper. Pity the poor GI who got three breakfasts instead of the desired combinations, but any veteran can tell you about always feeling hungry even after eating any K ration variation.

All three meals - breakfast, lunch and supper - had an emergency D ration bar which, was an unidentifiable solid bar with a cocoa-like smell containing nutrients and meant to be consumed after being dissolved in a canteen cup of water. Most GI's didn't bother and just bit into a crumbly cocoa-smelling something. It was after all solid food. One good thing about K rations, they were light and kept you alive, but the lack of bulk made the GIs always feel hungry.

"Boy, what I wouldn't give for a juicy cheeseburger right now," fantasized many field soldiers.

Surely, PVT Cavallo thought about his grandma's ravioli as he munched his K rations.

The army in its infinite wisdom always knew troops traveled on their stomachs and the better the chow, the better the soldier. All company-sized units of about 150 to 200 men had a mess section. The mess section leader was of course the mess sergeant, ruling with an iron hand over three or four cooks and the privates serving on KP duty that day.

The mess section set up a field kitchen to provide the men with hot meals and hot coffee. Field kitchens used gasoline to fire up the easily assembled combination stoves and ovens so they could be set up almost anywhere, even in the cargo bed of the army's workhorse truck, the

2½ ton, referred simply by the troops as the "deuce and a half. "

The chow was served while the troops lined up on a "chow line." The cooks and "KPs" (for the uninitiated KP stands for "Kitchen Police," a duty, performed daily by three or four privates on a rotating basis and sometimes for disciplinary purposes). The KPs stacked the food into the soldier's not too large individual mess kits. This at times gave a private with a grudge an opportunity to get back at his sergeant.

"Oops, sorry Sarge, didn't mean to pour the gravy for your dehydrated mashed potatoes all over your dessert but what the hell, you shouldn't mind. It's raining on your mess kit anyway ... Next!"

If you were lucky, sometimes by order of the CO, your mess sergeant would provide some warm water to shave with. Otherwise you shaved with cold water. Shaving was required for proper field sanitation in stateside training centers, but later on, in combat areas, there was to be little or no chance at all to shave with hot or cold water. Showers - well, that was a dream of a luxury that would have to wait for better times.

Chapter Three

2,500 Men Ready to Go

January 1944, with maneuvers behind them, all elements of the 97th Division were moved to Fort Leonard Wood, Missouri to prepare for deployment overseas to the Asiatic/Pacific Theater of operations. There is no doubt the 97th would be in line when and if the planned invasion of the Japanese home islands took place. The 97th Division enjoyed the reputation as one the best trained infantry divisions in the U.S. Army.

The troops were well trained to work as a team from the rifleman and his buddy up through the chain of command, with each man knowing his job and his responsibility. The combat commanders - from the corporals in charge of a mortar or machine gun sections, the squad and platoon sergeants, the lieutenants commanding the platoons and captains in charge of the infantry companies, and right on up to the 97th division commander - they were ready to go.

They were trained under the most realistic conditions as possible. But in war there is always the unexpected and, the unexpected happened to the 97th and of course, its men including my Cousin Vincent.

An order was received at Division Headquarters for the 97th Division to provide 5,000 officers and enlisted men for a much needed replacement pool. This depleted the division and drained a high percentage of the best trained men. The 5,000 men were divided into two groups of 2,500 each, one was selected to go to Burma, and Vincent was among that group. The other 2,500 men were sent to Europe to be trained for the forthcoming D-Day invasion of Normandy, France, on June 6th, 1944.

Here a pause is necessary to use some conjecture to determine why and how Vincent was selected to go with this particular group to Burma. We believe Vincent was among those who volunteered for a tougher assignment and here's why. First, his record showed he received a ten-day furlough from February 18th to February 28th. Then the furlough was mysteriously extended, and he received an additional five days to March 5th, 1944. This makes one wonder why this generous furlough was given to him at that time. Did the entire unit of 2,500 troops in Vincent's group get the same 15 days or, just the volunteers? This was unusual when the average furlough was much less time and a 15 day furlough unheard of for a GI on his way overseas to war.

Veterans tell of incentives to volunteer for more dangerous duty in exchange for some extra furlough time or even a promise for an early discharge. Vincent may have taken the gamble and volunteered to get his extra furlough time. Vincent Cavallo, Raymond's son, remembers his dad telling him about Vincent's time home during that furlough. Vincent told his brother Raymond that he was going on dangerous duty and may not be coming back. Also remembered is talk about one of Vincent's buddies visiting Vincent's parents after the war and telling them about how he also "volunteered" with Vincent. He further claimed to have been with Vincent when my cousin was killed in Myitkyina (incidentally, pronounced Mitch…inna).

My own memory of Vincent who was eight years my senior, was that he was remembered as a confident guy and probably would be a volunteer. Before my older brother Michael John passed away in 2005, we talked about Vincent. My brother was closer in age to Vincent and knew him better than I. My brother did not doubt for a moment, if given the opportunity Vincent would gamble for more furlough time and volunteer for something like this. Even, if it meant more dangerous duty. There was a time during my early research when I thought Vincent may have been with the original all volunteer 5307th 1st Galahad Force.

Surely at the time of his furlough, Vincent did not know his exact destination. He surely did not know he was going to Burma to serve with the badly needed replacements for the worn out and battered original brave 3,000 volunteers of the 1st Galahad force of Merrill's Marauders. Experience dictates that although rumors are wide-spread among the troops about their destination, there is always a chance someone may know something. Vincent could have heard or been told some information about an offer for volunteers for a more hazardous duty.

Research reveals Vincent's group of 2,500 men left on a troop train from Fort Leonard Wood, Missouri, on April 11th 1944. They traveled northeast, detrained and reported on April 13th to the Fort Meade, Maryland, Replacement Center. Now designated for security purposes, Casual Unit GH 770A, they awaited a troopship to carry them overseas.

These men were all well qualified infantrymen from a highly trained and proficient combat ready infantry division. Surely they all realized they were not being sent overseas to guard some warehouses out of harm's way and realized they would be seeing action. They were needed for a more dangerous mission; they just did not know at the time how dangerous their mission was going to be. Nor, how desperately they were needed, and, how quickly they would be facing the enemy's gun fire.

During that period of the war, most troops were sent to the European Theater of Operations (ETO) in preparation for the impending D-Day invasion of Europe. Other troops went to the Asiatic/Pacific Theater, which included China, Burma, and India (CBI). The ETO received most of the latest material, equipment, clothing, and food: the CBI was at the end of the supply line and got the leftovers. While Europe got quantities of the sleek, newer models of the P-51 Mustang fighter aircraft with the new clear, wide-vision bubble cockpits and the powerful P-47 Thunderbolt fighter planes, also with bubble cockpits, the CBI received only a few of the older P-51s and still used the even older Curtis P-40 fighter aircraft. All these aircraft had a dual purpose, both as fighters and also as attack planes to support the troops fighting on the ground.

The main emphasis was on the upcoming invasion of Europe, scheduled for June 6th, 1944. The CBI located at the extreme end of the supply line had to go to the back of the line for much of their needs. Men and material had to travel the longest distances to reach Burma. The

Allies' war plans at the time was a major effort for the war in Europe to defeat Germany first, then when victory was won in Europe, to concentrate on the destruction of Japan. Burma would just have to wait.

On April 23rd, 1944 U.S. Naval records revealed that Casual Unit GH 770A boarded the U.S. Navy armed troopship, USS General H. W. Butner, and departed Newport News, Virginia, at 2300 hours (11 PM). I read about one veteran of the GH 770A group who may or may not have known Vincent. He wrote about how they were told of their destination:

"The ship sailed into the Atlantic Ocean steering a course southeast, and after five days, the skipper and the army troop commander opened sealed orders and announced to the troops they would debark in Bombay, India (*now Mumbai*)"

The ship's first port of call was Cape Town, South Africa. Then the Butner traveled around the southern tip of Africa to stop at Durban, South Africa. Next, the Butner headed into the Indian Ocean and sailed north to Mombasa, Kenya, on the east coast of Africa.

After stopping at these distant seaports to load and unload cargo and troops and also refuel, the Butner continued in an easterly direction across the Indian Ocean towards India. Naval records further disclosed that the Butner either became part of a convoy or sailed singly under the escort of a British naval vessel, the HMS Tevkot Rocket, directly to Bombay. Other than some stormy seas along the way, there is no record of any enemy action on the voyage. The South Atlantic and Indian Oceans were still dangerous at that time and although very few in number, some enemy submarines were still operating in those waters.

The Butner was a fast U.S. Navy armed troop transport and because of its speed, may have travelled across the Atlantic Ocean alone without escort. The record shows it picked up the British escort equipped with anti-submarine detection devices and armaments for the last leg of the voyage through the Indian Ocean. The Butner's weapons consisted of four 5-inch naval dual purpose guns for use against surface as well as aerial targets. To protect against a low level air attack, it carried four quad-mount 1.1

inch antiaircraft guns and twenty single 20mm antiaircraft guns. These weapons were all manned by a U.S. Navy armed guard contingent who were there to operate the weapons. These U.S. sailors were all trained naval gunnery specialists.

With all this fire power aboard and experts to use it, the Butner was still vulnerable to an enemy submarine attack. At that phase of the war in 1944, an air attack was unlikely in the Indian Ocean but, an attack by enemy submarine was a distinct possibility. "Fire and boat drill" aboard ship was to train the troops to quickly assemble wearing their life preservers and then to report to the specific predetermined positions on the decks. They promptly collected on the upper decks where all the lifeboats and life rafts were located and made ready to be released if needed. This drill was practiced at the onset of the voyage and several times during the trip. This was to impress upon the troops the importance of a speedy assembly at their drill stations. It is certain the officers and men took these "fire and boat drills," very seriously.

After completing the voyage of approximately 13,000 miles, the Butner finally arrived in Bombay, India, on May 25th, 1944. Vincent debarked with all 2,500 troops from the Casual Unit 770A who were quickly assigned to their new unit, 2nd Galahad force 5307th Composite Unit Provisional.

At that time of the war, the troops going to Europe and arriving in the British Isles, received some weeks or even months of additional training and indoctrination before going into combat. Each man was paired with a buddy, and every officer and NCO knew their men and were trained to work as a team. There was no time for these important details for the men going to Burma.

The 2,500 destined as replacements for Merrill's 5307th were rushed directly into combat with no additional training. They would fight in a furious ongoing battle that began in mid-May and continued until August 3rd, 1944. These men were the replacements for the worn out and seriously depleted *Merrill's Marauders,* a name penned by a war correspondent after the unit's leader and newly promoted Brigadier General Frank Merrill.

Chapter Four

Merrill's Marauders

Prior to his promotion to a one star Brigadier, General Frank Merrill served on Lieutenant General Joseph Stilwell's staff in India and Burma. Merrill was promoted to General by Stilwell to command the original 1st Galahad 3,000-man force. Stilwell had a reputation for appointing his favorite people to important staff and command positions for which they were not totally trained. Merrill actually was a Cavalry officer, and although well-respected and an accomplished leader, he was however, not a very healthy person.

Merrill had two heart attacks during the Marauder's critical operations in Burma and had to be air-evacuated for medical treatment on both occasions. General Merrill's second heart attack occurred in the heat of the major battle at Myitkyina. Merrill made a wise choice for his next in command when he selected Lieutenant Colonel Charles Hunter whom he depended heavily upon to lead the Galahad force through all of their combat actions against the Japanese. Actually, Merrill spent some time with his command but perhaps spent too much of his time in Stilwell's headquarters, leaving Hunter in charge.

Hunter was a born leader and expert infantry tactician with years of service and led the Marauders through their most difficult times during the long trek and the violent sudden clashes with the enemy. It was Hunter and not Merrill who should have been given the greater credit for the unit's successes. This was because Merrill himself missed much of the rough march and close enemy actions the 5307th encountered on their way by foot to Myitkyina. Then after the force was badly depleted by the unknown and deadly jungle diseases, Hunter still led the attack on the airbase. Instead of giving the 5307th time to rest and get properly equipped and fed as promised, Stilwell ordered them again, to spearhead the attack on the town of Myitkyina. Many in the command believed this was another bad decision made by General Stilwell.

The Marauders' combat commanders included corporals and sergeants in charge of the machine gun and the mortar sections, and the riflemen squads and platoons. Together with the platoon officers and the company commanders they all lived and battled the enemy side by side. They ate the same rations, endured the same hardships and dangers, and were exposed and stricken by the same diseases and violent enemy actions. General Merrill was absent from most of the hardships of sudden close combat and the perils the Marauders were faced with. He spent a good deal of his time at headquarters or recovering from two heart attacks, and then serving in British Lord Louis Mountbatten's headquarters in India. This was proven by the massive materiel I read, researched, and studied. I listed this material in the bibliography at the end of this narrative to make it available for the reader. This material revealed to me that the 5307th should have been managed and supplied much better than their headquarters thought necessary. The 3,000 man 1st Galahad Force was divided into three battalions each led by an excellent infantry Major equally responsible to Hunter for the success of their mission in Burma.

The recognition and credit for his ability and leadership was denied Hunter because, he was simply not a "yes man." He reported truthfully and competently to Merrill and then directly to Stilwell when Merrill was recovering from his heart attacks and not available to his second in command. My research also goes a step further, exposing Merrill's desire to agree with everything Stilwell espoused. Maybe Merrill felt he owed so much to Stilwell or that he truly believed Stilwell was infallible. I do not recall reading at any time Merrill ever questioning any of Stilwell's decisions or, ever questioning any of Stilwell's staff for their continuing errors and misjudgments. Instead, Merrill appeared to take the side of Stilwell's staff who considered Hunter to be a complainer.

The most profound failure was not realizing or trying to find out what dangers the men of the Galahad force were to face in the Burmese jungles. Stilwell's staff failed to recognize how important a more nutritious diet was which alone, caused the loss of most of the original force to sickness and disease. I could not find a single time when Stilwell's staff asked British General Orde Wingate his opinions on anything. Wingate's Chindits went through exactly what the 5307th was about to experience. It was no secret that Stilwell did not like the British, so no help or advice was forthcoming from that valuable source.

Why was Merrill not relieved when he had his first heart attack, particularly in such an unhealthy and threatening environment as Burma? My God, Merrill had a heart condition, and Stilwell effectively did nothing about it. Any other commander would have relieved Merrill and promoted Hunter to a full colonel to continue his excellent successes thus far.

Stilwell's insistence together with Chief of Staff General Marshall's support for Stilwell's stubborn demands were finally met. Now, Stilwell was given full command of the 5307th. This was proven to be the first step toward disaster for the unit. Our brave soldiers were sent into the Burmese jungle well trained and well-armed for their mission but very poorly equipped and fed. They were issued pup tents instead of the available and much more essential jungle hammocks with sand fly netting and rain covers to keep the troops from sleeping on the infected ground. Stilwell's staff apparently knew nothing about the perils of the Burmese jungle. In addition, the troops were poorly advised on such particularly important matters as drinking water discipline on the trail.

In February 1944, 2,750 healthy well-trained and well-armed American soldiers of the 5307th entered Burma. In only just a few months' time, about 300 sick and tattered malaria and dysentery stricken men were fit for duty from the original unit. Upon receiving orders from his boss General Stilwell, Merrill ordered his second in command, Lieutenant Colonel Hunter, to spearhead a major attack on Myitkyina with his few remaining troops. This was after Merrill made an unfulfilled promise to the men of the 5307th to be relieved to rest, eat some hot meals and recuperate for a very short rest period before the next combat action.

Merrill also promised Hunter he would be the first off the plane to meet Hunter at the airbase in Myitkyina and that Merrill himself would then take over the stresses of command from Hunter. The men were given the order and steeled themselves again to go on with the mission. Their *esprit de corps* starting to wane. Merrill never showed up at the airbase as he promised he would, which left Hunter with a group of worn out, sick and diseased tormented but still brave warriors to continue the fight.

Chapter Five

3,000 American Volunteers

The original 5307th was created in 1943 by a promise President Franklin Roosevelt made to the British Prime Minister, Winston Churchill when both met at the Quebec Conference hosted by Canada. One topic was the war in Burma that the British were fighting. Roosevelt promised to send a unit for deep-penetration, Ranger-style action to assist the British in Burma. The plan was to create a force of 3,000 infantrymen to form an all-American volunteer combat force to fight in Burma alongside the Chinese and British Commonwealth forces and native units. The Americans would have the more dangerous assignment to spearhead the thrust forward to attack and then occupy the enemy airbase at Myitkyina. They were to be the very first U.S. ground combat troops to fight on the continent of Asia during World War II.

Roosevelt had no idea the hardships these men would experience during their short but dangerous and yes, tragic mission. Almost the entire unit was lost mainly to disease rather than battle casualties. The jungle diseases were the unseen enemy that the planners failed to recognize and to provide some common-sense prevention which, Stilwell's staff should have considered. Again, the unexpected!

This lack of reasonable foresight became a serious challenge for all the army medical corps people in the area. During the operation, men were evacuated with open sores that would not heal and with high fevers that would not respond to any known treatment. Diagnosis was uncertain, and the medics simply classified these debilitating diseases resulting in many cases to tragic deaths to, "Disease of Unknown Origin" or more simply stated for the records, "DUO." No records could be found which reported how many men actually died from DUO while still in field hospitals in Burma and India.

The original 5307th 1st Galahad was a unit of regimental strength made up of three battalions totaling about 3,000 men who were assembled soon after Roosevelt's promise to the British. The order called for volunteers for "hazardous duty in a jungle area." One battalion was recruited from combat units who fought at Guadalcanal and other islands in the Pacific, another group from units stationed in tropical areas in the Caribbean and, one unit from soldiers training in the United States. One veteran tells of the incentives offered to him if he volunteered. He was promised a furlough and early release from active duty. He got neither, and in his eighties when I spoke to him on the phone, he was thankful to have survived the ordeal.

The volunteers of the 5307th 1st Galahad arrived in Bombay, India, on October 31st, 1943. They trained in India with British Chindit units, a British unit with experience fighting behind the enemy lines in Burma under the command of British General Orde Wingate. (Chindit origin: Chinthe, a mythical Burmese lion or some reference to the Chindwin River).

The Chindits were the perfect advisors for the 5307th, but Stilwell disproved of the American force joining with the British and under their tactical control. Stilwell demanded the direct command of the 5307th. This was to prove to be a grave misfortune for the Marauders.

The 5307th divided the force into three battalions with each battalion commanded by very competent infantry majors. Each battalion was evenly composed of combat veterans, new men from the training centers and those men having experience in the jungle and tropical environments. Each battalion trained to peak efficiency and established cohesiveness that assured *Esprit de Corps* and each man knew he was an important part of a unified team.

They trained for a three month period in Northern India and then in early February 1944, they marched out of India into Northern Burma. The mission was to be a top secret operation but, the Japanese army had many sympathizers and collaborators in India. It is reported that when the Galahad Force crossed the border on foot into Northern Burma and stopped the first night to rest and bivouac, the radio operators were surprised to hear *Tokyo Rose* welcoming the 5307th to Burma. The enemy knew the Marauders were at their doorstep, again the unexpected.

Both Burma and India were British colonies bordering each other. Earlier in the war, the Japanese occupied Burma and closed the Burma Road. This was the Allies' main supply lifeline to Nationalist China to bring them the much needed war materials. It was the Allies' wish to keep the Chinese in the war against Japan to help slow down further enemy expansion in that part of Asia. They did not want the Chinese to make a separate peace treaty with Japan. This would have released many thousands of Japanese troops to fight against the Allies mainly, the American forces fighting in the Pacific theater. This would have slowed down our advances and prolonged the war indefinitely.

The Burma Road was now occupied by the Imperial Japanese forces and closed for use to the Allies who were now supplying the Chinese by air from India. At the same time the U.S. Army engineers were hacking out of the jungles and mountains of Burma a new supply route called, The Ledo Road.

The U.S. Army Air Corp used twin engine Curtis C-46 and Douglas C-47 Cargo planes flying from India to bring a continual flow of supplies to bases in Western China. This area was still free from the Japanese invaders and under the control of Chinese Generalissimo Chiang Kei Shek's Nationalist Forces.

The cargo planes were unarmed and flew with a crew of five. The pilot, co-pilot, and navigator were officer's usually first or second lieutenants and if they survived long enough, some were promoted to captain. The radio operator and the "kicker" to handle the cargo were all corporals or sergeants. The Japanese Air Forces having air superiority were able to intercept and shoot down our cargo planes with impunity. This forced the air commanders to reroute the cargo planes further and further to the north, over the treacherous Himalayan Mountains, the highest in the world. Flying the "Hump" was some of the most challenging flying experiences for those young pilots and crews.

The Allies had fighter planes in the CBI Theater but, they were based too far away in India or in air bases deep in China that were still out of reach of the Japanese enemy. At that time the fighters did not have the capability to fly as escorts at such distances and at such high altitudes for prolonged periods of flight time.

Many cargo planes were lost to enemy fighter interception, enemy ground antiaircraft artillery fire, and far too many to pilot error and equipment failure. Of the two planes, the Curtis C-46s were least reliable, whereas the Douglas C-47s were the more dependable. The C-47's later became even more famous in civilian aviation, as the DC-3 commercial air liner. The Curtis C-46s had a much greater cargo capacity which motivated the military to rush them into service. This was to satisfy the Nationalist Chinese leader Chiang Kei Shek's demand for more supplies.

The problems with the C-46s had to be human engineered by the ground crews in India. Many crews were forced to abandon ship and parachute into the forbidding jungles of Burma. Very few were rescued and returned to duty by OSS-trained Kachin tribesman. Most were lost to the jungle or were captured and executed by Japanese soldiers. We can only imagine how unnerving it must have been for those young pilots and their air crews to fly over hostile landscape littered with the wreckage of crashed planes recently flown by their comrades.

The main objective for the 5307th's mission was to spearhead the combined allied Chinese and British Commonwealth forces including the Indian and Gurkha troops to capture the airbase and town of Myitkyina. This town was strategically located at the terminus of the Mandalay to Myitkyina Railroad and, the Irrawaddy River. Myitkyina was the only all-weather air base in North Burma. This entire area was heavily fortified and occupied by the Japanese forces. The enemy fighter aircraft operating out of this air base controlled the skies over Northern Burma. They easily devastated the slow flying unarmed and unescorted cargo planes.

Myitkyina was a transportation hub with access by both air and rail which gave the Japanese a distinct advantage over the Allies. Myitkyina had to be taken and occupied, and the 5307th was to lead the way with a terribly depleted force. This was not fully realized by Stilwell and his incompetent staff. The festering tragedy overlooked by Stilwell and his poorly-chosen staff sent 2,750 brave and combat-ready American soldiers into a grossly misjudged quagmire of dangers.

These brave volunteers were led into combat by the highly competent second in command, Lieutenant Colonel Charles Newton Hunter. This officer was a graduate of the U.S. Army Ranger School and well qualified for the job. This is when the leader Brigadier General Merrill was recovering at headquarters from two heart attacks. Stilwell's indifferent staff continued doing a terrible job in supporting these volunteers and provided them with faulty intelligence and poor operational support in the field. Stilwell's staff failed to supply the 5307th with special jungle hammocks with sand fly netting and rain covers and, to provide the proper rations another unconscionable error. Apparently the staff was allowed to function without any oversight by Stilwell himself. These factors alone were the most damning disasters that brought debilitating sickness and avoidable death to the brave soldiers who volunteered for this mission.

The operational plan was for the 5307th' to penetrate on foot into Burma using mules and horses to carry their equipment. Once behind the Japanese lines, they were to disrupt enemy communications and cause as much havoc as possible. They were to fight their way through Northern Burma to Myitkyina. The objective was to take the air base first and then the town of Myitkyina. On the way they were to be supplied by airdrops.

Originally the 5307th was to be placed under the command of British Lord Louis Mountbatten, who was the appointed Supreme Commanding Officer of all allied forces in the CBI. This was the same status General Dwight Eisenhower had as the Supreme Commander of all allied forces in Europe.

The 5307th was to serve under the tactical field command of British General Orde Wingate, a very eccentric, although most competent and experienced officer, who wrote the book on long range penetration tactics. This was exactly what the 5307th was sent to Burma to do. Wingate had a great deal of firsthand experience in Burma with his Chindit Force and had already launched operations behind the enemy lines in Burma and knew the dangers.

Wingate's Chindit force had already experienced the problems that would face the 5307th and could have given invaluable advice to Stilwell and Merrill. Wingate had vast experience in other underdeveloped areas in the world and could have offered vital help to sustain the combat effectiveness of the Marauders. He was to train the 5307th and participate in the tactical planning. After all, he was the perfect advisor for General Merrill and Colonel Hunter. Instead, Stilwell decided to deprive the 5307th of this invaluable help and for personal reasons insisted on placing the

1st Galahad brave volunteers under his direct command.

U.S. Lieutenant General Joseph Stilwell was nicknamed “Vinegar Joe” because of his cantankerous disposition. He was the area commander for all U.S. and Chinese troops and reluctantly subordinate to Lord Mountbatten. Stilwell insisted upon bringing the 5307th under his direct command, which he finally achieved. All writings by participants suggest Stilwell should have paid closer attention to the details of the operation instead, he left the details up to his less than competent staff officers. This was to cause the 5307th much unnecessary anguish, pain, and suffering. Stilwell’s G-3 Operations Officer should have paid more attention to the planning phase. Particularly, the mountainous terrain, jungles, and river obstacles the troops had to travel though which, was totally overlooked. Wingate’s advice was not asked by the Americans because Stilwell felt he did not need the British.

The G-4 Supply Officer should have found the special jungle hammocks stored in a warehouse in India and overlooked until it was too late. These hammocks would have kept the troops off the ground and given them protection against the many diseases carried by the deadly microbes that literally infected the Burmese jungles of rotting vegetation and animal matter. These conditions infected the troops simply by their sleeping on the ground, and Wingate's force knew this. Almost all the Galahad force soldiers suffered from malaria and dysentery.

Scrub typhus was a deadly disease, and no records were kept that I could find to tell how many well-trained and healthy Marauders met and were killed by this microbe. They were catching up on some well-needed shuteye by sleeping on the wet, putrid jungle ground.

This threat was unknown to our forces and a tragedy that could have been easily avoided possibly by a friendly drink a "Limey" sergeant had with a "Yank" sergeant at an NCO club, or even possibly an American officer sipping a gin and tonic with Wingate himself at an officers' club. This of course, is just a fantasy. Plus, Wingate was kind of quirky and somewhat of a loner, but the idea is feasible. I recall having drinks in Korea with Australian sergeants talking about their experiences against the enemy. And, there was plenty of fraternization between the Allies in all ranks and in all theaters of war in World War II, even in the CBI! Some of these "clubs" were no more than a few wooden boards thrown across two empty 55-gallon diesel oil fuel barrels within the sound of artillery fire.

But, "Vinegar Joe" did not want any collaboration with the British, and when the 5307th took the airbase at Myitkyina, Lord Louis Mountbatten was surprised. He was shocked that Stilwell did not confer with his immediate commanding officer about the action until the airbase was captured. The few remaining original Marauders were exhausted. Reports were filed about some men so sick and fatigued from severe cases of dysentery that they could not stop defecating in their pants. In Barbara W. Tuchman's book, *Stilwell and the American Experience in China,* she states on page 538 "they cut away the seat of their pants." It is all there for the readers and, Wingate's Chindits Force also had similar experiences. But, Stilwell was still laughing at the "Limeys" when, the airbase at Myitkyina was captured with the Marauders spearheading the action without Mountbatten's knowledge.

Everyone on Stilwell's staff knew K rations were designed for consumption no longer than five days at a time and were emergency survival or combat rations only. C rations, although heavier to transport, were much more nutritious and also available, and G-4 should have supplied them more freely. If anyone was even paying attention, it was common knowledge that a steady diet of K rations will rob the body of essential nutrients so necessary for the body to combat the many diseases of the Burmese jungles.

Last but not least were the errors of the intelligence staff under Colonel Joseph Stilwell, Jr., "Vinegar Joe's" son, the G-2 intelligence officer. They were wrong time and time again by underestimating many aspects of intelligence about the enemy, a most deadly deficiency. There were also special American

OSS Detachment 101 operatives on the ground in North Burma. These operatives were working with the local and friendly Kachin tribesmen who hated the Japanese.

Although Colonel Hunter made contact with and received help from Detachment 101 units, G-2 should have made better use of these assets, particularly with respect to the enemy's strength and capabilities. Detachment 101 had boots and eyes on the ground and should have been better used by the planners in Stilwell's headquarters.

General Stilwell had little regard for OSS (Office of Strategic Services) personnel and their leader, General William Donovan. Stilwell resented the popular and colorful "Wild Bill," Donovan Medal of Honor recipient from World War I. Donavan successfully placed thousands of trained intelligence gatherers throughout the world. This boosted our allied planner's ability to read the enemies intentions and was welcomed by the military tacticians. But, this was just not fully understood by the pragmatic hardheaded old infantryman "Vinegar Joe Stilwell."

Lieutenant Colonel Charles Hunter wrote a scathing report about the failure of Stilwell's staff on these important details. This later blemished Hunter's career. The report went on to state, "The force was dissipated by tropical disease made worse from a constant diet of K rations." Hunter sent a steady flow of Galahad's needs to the staff and reported the staff's failures to Stilwell. Stilwell recoiled from Hunter's request for promised and well-deserved promotions and medals for his troops by telling Hunter, "The 5307th should be doing more fighting and less complaining about medals and promotions." This is after the troops had lost most of the men to disease and the strain of close combat for months without a break. Constant contact with the enemy on lonely trails with some fire fights at distances of only 50 yards from the unseen enemy in the dense Burmese jungles.

General Merrill spent quite a bit of time with Stilwell and less time in the field with the Marauders, which caused him to lose the respect of some of the troops in Galahad. My research hinted that many in the area were beginning to think Merrill was a "yes man" to Stilwell.

The men in the 5307th had to walk and fight for over 700 miles before reaching the main objective at Myitkyina. The unit then had to engage the enemy in a major battle. From the starting point at Ledo, India, to Myitkyina, Burma, it appeared on maps to be only a few hundred miles as the crow flies. The troops did not fly instead, they had to climb up many mountains and then slide and stumble back down into the wet and humid jungle valleys. Each step adding miles to the distance traveled. If Stilwell's staff or Stilwell himself or for that matter any soldier, looked closer at the topographical maps the distance would have been more accurately determined. The contour lines on all military topographic maps show mountain steepness and altitude. The distance could easily have been estimated...The closer the lines the steeper the mountain. Burma was a British colony for years and the area must have been mapped by them. How could Stilwell's staff have missed that basic soldierly skill? Every soldier is schooled in map reading so, there is no excuse for this oversight

G-3 should have worked closer with G-2 for better knowledge and understanding of the terrain. They should have depended more on Detachment 101 and for that matter, British General Wingate's people who had boots on the ground and vast experience in Burma. Certainly, Stilwell's son, the G-2 intelligence officer could have easily coordinated closer with the OSS people and assigned more and willing Detachment 101 men and Kachin tribesman to help. They were ready and willing to act as advisors and guides and to assist Galahad with commonsense jungle field practices. There was also a British infantry unit close enough for help with additional and much needed troops. But Stilwell insisted, "The Limeys are mad, so let's just leave them alone." Stilwell did not want to the share the credit with the British when his forces took the airbase at Myitkyina and later the village from the Japanese.

Chiang Kei Shek requested Roosevelt to relieve Stilwell many times over a long period of time and, Washington was reluctant until Stilwell was finally relieved and returned to the states. Many in the command thought Stilwell was the least effective officer to have been given such an immensely important military and diplomatic responsibility and much has been written negatively about him in this regard.

The unit's only transport were pack animals for which the individual Marauder had little pack animal training. The pack animals were to carry their extra ammunition, food, crew-served weapons and the important radios. The radios were essential for continual contact with headquarters and the supply planes. To further complicate the mission, the cargo ship with the trained animals and animal handler personnel was torpedoed by the Japanese and never made it to India and to the 5307th in the field. Stilwell should have had contingency plans, which were apparently non-existent.

It is wiser to "BE prepared" than wait for an emergency and then try to catch up to "GET prepared."

General Stilwell should have asked his son, the Intelligence Officer: "How accurate are the intelligence estimates? From what sources are you gathering intelligence about the enemy? Have you ever met with and verified this with Detachment 101 commanders on the ground?"

Stilwell should have asked his G-3 operations officer, "Have your people analyzed the topography? Has 101 been asked to help, they are already there and know the country? Has Hunter been advised with your best information?"

General Merrill should have paid closer attention to Hunter's requests and saw to it that they were fulfilled. This is how a combat commander deals with his staff rather than assume all is well. Any "green" 2nd lieutenant taking the Army Leadership Correspondence Courses would know to ask those important questions. Stilwell had more than a cursory military education after graduating 32nd in a class of 124 at West Point in 1904 and should have known better. He should have given more thought to leaving the 5307th under British command for training and tactics and concentrated on providing the 5307th with proper food rations, equipment, and supplies.

The British under Wingate had already experienced the hardships of combat operations on the trail in the Northern Burmese jungles. Wingate's men would have warned 5307th and this would have prevented many of the adversities caused by the microbes that tore the Galahad force to pieces. Wingate saw what his own Chindit forces suffered.

The troops had to climb mountains, ford rivers and hack their way through impenetrable monsoon-drenched jungles. This is while being fed non-nutritional K rations as their main diet which, caused the greatest damage to the men's health.

In spite of all the shortcomings, the 5307th fought and won five major and thirty minor battles against superior enemy forces of well-trained and well-fed soldiers if, you liked eating snake meat with your rice ration. The opposing Japanese forces at Myitkyina were a mix of several units some were from the Japanese 18th Division. This was the very same force that conquered Malaysia and Singapore the British imagined invincible fortress at the tip of the Malay Peninsula.

Singapore was fortified against an expected attack from the sea but, the Japanese surprised the British and attacked from the jungles. They found the British to be totally unprepared for an assault from the jungle, and the battle ended when the British surrendered "Fortress Singapore" to the Japanese. The Japanese encouraged their soldiers to eat snake meat, a readily available and nutritious source of protein.

The monsoon season delivered a deluge of unending rain pouring on the troops. The driving torrential rains turned jungle trails into rivers. The British Lord Louis Mountbatten while on a reconnaissance flight over Burma, asked the pilot to identify the river below. The pilot replied they had just flown over the new Ledo Road. This was monsoon season when the roads turned into muddy rivers. At the end of the rainy season, the humidity was choking and it seemed leeches were found under almost every leaf in the Burmese jungle.

The Marauders traveled the world's most uninhabitable geography on foot. They crossed rivers and climbed up and then slid down the steep mountains for over 500 miles. This included their trek from within India to the North Burma border. The actual distance the 5307th traveled is still not agreed upon.

The Galahad Force finally arrived at their major objective of Myitkyina and the enemy air base. Much less than a third of the original roughly 2,700 member Galahad Force were still on their feet sick, but still standing. The records vary, but only about 300 men were actually fit for duty, and here again the responsibility fell squarely on Stilwell's shoulders.

During the trek to Myitkyina, the sick and wounded were air evacuated on small single-engine planes flying from airstrips hacked out of the jungles by the 5307th. The sick and injured men were flown back to field hospitals in Burma and India. Of the original force entering Burma, 93 were killed in combat, an additional 30 killed in accidents, 293 wounded, 8 missing in action, and the rest evacuated due to sickness and disease. This left only a few hundred to spearhead the attack on the town of Myitkyina.

While fighting continued at Myitkyina, General Stilwell ordered the medical units to release for duty as many sick and wounded as possible. Colonel Hunter desperately needed help at Myitkyina but, Stilwell would not alert that nearby British infantry unit that could have offered help to the Marauders.

I cannot understand the thinking at that time at Stilwell's headquarters. Our army was known to be the best fed army in the world and, C rations and other nutritious rations were plentiful throughout all combat areas in 1944 including, the CBI.

The planners should have paid more attention to these details and considered the unexpected which, will always occur in a fluid dynamic operation such as the mission given the 5307th. Better planning would have kept more troops out of hospitals because of sickness. Some reports tell of Galahad troops simply swallowing a water purification tablet and then drinking water right from a stream, thinking it would kill the bugs in the water. They should have been trained to first fill their one quart canteen with water then drop in one or two purification tablets, shake it up to dissolve the purifying chemicals and then, drink the water. This bit of instruction alone would have saved many from the debilitating, and in too many cases, deadly jungle diseases. Had the unit remained under Wingate's command, they would have been warned about proper drinking water discipline. I searched but could not find any numbers of the men who later died of their disease after they were evacuated.

Where were the planners? Why didn't they pass this information down to the GI who was on the front line? The unit was losing more men from disease than were killed and wounded in combat. Stilwell's staff had plenty of purified water to drink at their headquarters and probably something a little stronger to go along with it. It is also doubtful to think the staff dined on U.S. Army Ration K every day as the Marauders did. From what has been written about Stilwell himself, he probably did eat Ks the same as the troops did. But, there is no excuse for ignoring the details and the resulting unexpected hardships on his men. A good commander always prepares for the worst-case scenario and makes alternate plans for his troops to deal with the unexpected.

My research reveals Stilwell left too many decisions to others and should have paid closer personal attention to the details or, as most smart combat commanders did, appoint a proficient detail man to work with the staff to spot and correct these deficiencies.

Remember the small details…a flash to the troops before they were sent out… "Advise troops to purify water in canteen before drinking." This admonition alone would have saved many of the DUO casualties. Stilwell's plate was already full with his primary mission to train the Chinese army and, he should not have demanded command of the Galahad Force. This was wrong because the well-defined mission for the 5307th was more in line with today's Special Forces. And, British General Ord Wingate was the expert with experience in Burma for long-range deep penetration operations into enemy territory. It is too bad General Stilwell did not coordinate and take advantage of the valuable British assets available to him and his command.

General Merrill had to be air-evacuated during the fierce fighting in Myitkyina. This left Lieutenant Colonel Hunter to command the operations which, actually assured the success. I cannot imagine why Stilwell did not relieve Merrill from active duty in the field after his first heart attack. Merrill's heart condition should have prevented him from even serving in such a torturous climate as Burma and, the demanding role of commanding the 5307th. This was more of a political decision than a military one by Stilwell who felt more comfortable with Merrill and perhaps, Merrill was more malleable for Stilwell to work with. I think Stilwell preferred…"Yes, sir" from his subordinates rather than, "Sir, I think we should try to do it this way and here are my reasons why."

In May 1944, together with a large force of mostly Chinese and some mixed British Commonwealth forces, Stilwell ordered the small and depleted Galahad Force to spearhead the attack on the town of Myitkyina. The allies succeeded in taking the Japanese-held airbase, which was a major victory while, the battle for the town was becoming more and more desperate. However, the area commander, Lord Louis Mountbatten, was completely in the dark and was surprised when the victory at Myitkyina was announced by Stilwell. "Vinegar Joe" loved to keep the "Limeys" guessing.

The popular American expression of "SNAFU" (Situation Normal All Fouled Up) may have originated in the CBI and, the word "Fouled" up was never used in practice. The G-3 intelligence people informed Galahad that they would be facing a much smaller enemy force of poorly trained garrison troops left to defend Myitkyina. This was only partially true when it was found there were over 4,600 enemy troops some well-trained and most well-fed and equipped. Also some combat veterans, from the 18th Division the "Singapore Victors," were there defending the town of Myitkyina. The enemy made some critical intelligence mistakes also by over-estimating our forces. The Japanese commanders failed to exploit several chances to overwhelm the positions held by the attacking allied troops.

Although hundreds of Chinese soldiers fought and died bravely, their leadership was not the best. This was another failure resting squarely on the shoulders of General Stilwell. He was responsible for the training of all Chinese forces in the area. He served in China as a young officer and spoke some Chinese dialects very well. He should have placed 100% of his effort to turning out an exemplary Chinese army instead of involving his time and effort with Galahad. He was then further remiss in proper supervision of his selected staff, including his son, Lieutenant Colonel Joseph Stilwell, Jr., the staff intelligence officer.

Young Stilwell misread the enemy's strength time after time. Maybe General Marshall, the army chief of staff back in Washington, should have taken a closer look into the China, Burma, and India Theater after hearing numerous complaints about Stilwell.

Marshall knew "Vinegar Joe'" was no Eisenhower.

General Marshall should have demanded Roosevelt release him to travel to the troubled CBI area to see for himself the compounding of errors. The president did not want Marshall to be away from his side, and Marshall remained to stay close to our ailing President Roosevelt while the President was still alive.

The Supreme Commander of the European Theater of Operations was well led by Dwight D. Eisenhower who knew how to deal with the allied prima donnas, like British Field Marshall Montgomery without insulting them. Stilwell did not possess the special and necessary common sense and tact to succeed in the military and in the diplomatic position that was forced upon him.

The 5307th's spearhead at Myitkyina was starting to get blunted when it was discovered that the Commander of a much needed Chinese pack artillery unit discarded some of their 75mm shells and the batteries for their radios. The Chinese commander decided they were just too heavy for his troops to carry through the steaming jungles. Communication is essential for accurate artillery fire, and refusing to carry extra ammo unpardonable.

Stilwell was responsible for the training and was in command of all the Chinese forces in the theater. Chinese soldiers were brave and excellent troops when led by competent and aggressive Chinese officers.

The Japanese were dug in and were in excellent positions to defend Myitkyina and out-gunned the Allies with greater numbers of much heavier artillery precisely zeroed in on allied positions. Japanese artillery set up a constant barrage and concentration of fire on our troops. The battle turned into a World War I type of trench warfare, and the Marauders were too lightly armed for this type of fighting. They were effectively armed for their specific mission of movement behind the enemy's lines. In this type of a siege battle, the heaviest artillery usually wins. These troops had a limited number of light artillery, 75mm pack howitzers and only one 155mm gun to use against the more numerous Japanese medium and heavy artillery 105mm and 150mm howitzers.

Howitzer artillery tactics aim the guns at a high angle. The shells are shot at a high arc over any hills to come plummeting down on the enemy force on the other side of the hill. Allied air support was limited but very effective, only it was too little and too late. I read about a P-51 pilot who kept his one and only plane ready at Myitkyina to support the attack. He worked closely with Galahad until the pilot's bombs and .50 caliber machinegun ammunition was expended. It was also too little and too late.

Unlike the bloody battles on Iwo Jima and Okinawa where the marines and army had the support of heavy naval guns and superior air forces, the troops in Myitkyina were armed with very light weaponry. The Japanese were determined not only to hold the town of Myitkyina but to retake the air base. This was a desperate move in a desperate battle that could go either way. The Marauders needed infantry replacements and they needed them fast….very fast.

Hunter relates a bitter disappointment when his request for infantry replacements were assured by Stilwell's headquarters that a glider force was that very moment in the air and on the way to Myitkyina. When these forces arrived, they turned out to be an Army aviation engineer unit with orders and tools to repair the airfield that did not need repairing. The engineers soon had to abandon their tools and fight as infantry which, they did gallantly, but it still was not enough. Another example of yet another SNAFU made by Stilwell's G-3 operations people. The situation was getting much worse as the clouds darkened over Myitkyina and the 5307th. Hunter did not know at the time that the army was already dispatching a replacement force for the badly battered and diminished 1st Galahad with a fresh force of troops, code named 2nd Galahad.

Chapter Six

2nd Galahad Arrives

On May 25th, 1944 the General H. W. Butner arrived in Bombay, India. Thousands of troops and tons of supplies were off-loaded for the buildup in the China, Burma, and India Command. The 2,500 casual troops, identified as GH 770A, were destined for replacements for the decimated Merrill's Marauders.

The replacements were quickly loaded on trains and were rushed to an air base in Northern India and the 2,500 troops were now given the new name of the 5307th Composite Unit Provisional code named 2nd Galahad. These replacements were immediately rushed to Myitkyina with no time for indoctrination to the area or the mission. The officers and NCOs did not know who their men would be nor any word on the mission. They were speedily loaded on C-46 and C-47 cargo planes or on gliders towed by these planes and flown directly to the air base in Myitkyina. Upon arriving they were met by the unrelenting pounding of enemy artillery and small arms fire. They were rapidly formed into platoons and companies to face the enemy.

As the Lieutenants and Captains stepped out of those planes and gliders they were ordered to command platoons and companies to lead men mostly unknown to them, a poor start indeed.

Vincent was assigned to F Company 2nd Galahad. His Morning Report Locator Card shows he reported to the 5307th Comp Unit, Provisional on 1 June, 1944. Private Cavallo entered hell on earth when his boots hit the ground at the Myitkyina air base.

Somewhere along the way to Myitkyina, Vincent and his comrades were given a combat issue of ammunition for their weapons, K rations, and water for their canteens. Their weapons were both the M1 rifle and 1903 Springfield rifle, a few 1903A4 Springfield sniper rifles with telescope sights. Also issued were the M1 carbine, Browning automatic rifle (BAR) and the Thompson and the M-3 submachine guns. Some men operating the Browning machine gun and the 60mm mortars were issued .45 caliber automatic pistols which were also issued to the officers. The 2.36 inch bazooka and the bulky rocket ammo was also listed but, I did not find any mention of the bazooka being used. Hand grenades were also made available and this comprised the infantry armaments issued to the 2nd Galahad force.

Vincent entered the hotly contested battle for the town of Myitkyina. There were no pauses in the battle which kept Vincent in close contact with the enemy until he was killed on June 28th, 1944. He was in 2nd Galahad for just 27 days, fighting in very close combat without any relief in sight when his days on earth ended.

What caused some confusion in my research was the receipt of a copy of the 52B form that was attached to Vincent's remains, and again some guesswork here. The 52B medical form used by the army medical corps is pictured at the end of this narrative. This hints that Vincent may have been wounded and recovered from the battlefield while still alive. Then, he may have been carried to one of three field hospitals at the airfield. The 52B form is signed by what appears to be Major Wendell L. Spalding, Medical Corps. I searched for this name in the three field hospitals with no success. The specific purpose for issuing two GI dog tags the soldier must wear around his neck, is to place one on the deceased and the other to be retained by the unit to keep a record of those killed in action. Vincent's 52 B form reads, "PVT Vincent Cavallo, Serial Number 32XXXXXX" F Company 2nd Galahad, "all hurriedly written down in pencil. It simply states. "Killed in action in line of duty." Vincent was 19 years old and would have been 20 in October, 1944.

The battle for Myitkyina lasted until the beginning of August 1944, and shortly after that the 5307th was disbanded. No one knows how the morning reports, the after-action reports, and personnel records were handled. This is one of the reasons Vincent's personnel record is so incomplete. God only knows if Vincent's squad leader, platoon sergeant, platoon leader, or the F Company commander even survived the battle. For all we know he may even have been promoted on the spot by a platoon sergeant or officer as men dropped in combat and others were called upon to carry on. And yes, teenagers did step up to the challenge and did lead men only now, they were no longer teens just out of high school but men! I imagine it happened in the heat and confusion of battle for a startled young private to look at an officer pointing his finger at him and shouting, "You are now in charge, sergeant," as they both ran for cover.

The most decorated hero of World War II was Audie Murphy. He enlisted in the regular army as a private when he was 17 years old after being turned down by the marines for being under weight. At war's end in 1945, he was honorably discharged as a 20-year-old lieutenant having served in the fighting in Italy and France in the 3rd and 36th Infantry Divisions. He was promoted on the spot from private to sergeant under those very same set of circumstances I described. After many more heroic deeds in the war and additional awards, he received our nation's highest decoration for gallantry in action, "The Congressional Medal of Honor." He also received a battlefield commission to second lieutenant. He survived the war and had an acting career in Hollywood and was later killed in a civilian plane accident. His life is an interesting read. But, I doubt if his name is even known by many today.

The 2nd Galahad Force was hastily formed on the battlefield and the leaders didn't even know the names of their own men. This was not a proud moment for those who planned this operation, and it was poorly recorded by the army.

I have dug deep so far unsuccessfully, for details about F Company 2nd Galahad. General "Vinegar Joe" Stilwell was not alone when he wrote his wife that he was thankful the Battle of Myitkyina, or as it was recorded for the history books, "The Siege of Myitkyina" was over.

Much was written about Merrill's Marauders, and I have read and studied a vast amount of material about its short history from November 1943 to August 1944. The data about 2nd Galahad and its action at Myitkyina are somewhat sketchy. The information in this book was obtained by reading interesting and detailed volumes about the Marauders and researching army records from many sources, information gleaned from the internet, and by interviewing a veteran of 1st Galahad who was there. He asked that his name not be used which, I have honored. This veteran did not know many men in the 2nd Galahad Force and did not know my cousin, Private Cavallo.

I am still researching their role and how much they endured during the battle. Without the 2,500 urgently needed men of the 2nd Galahad force being present at that momentous time, there is no question that the enemy would have recaptured the air base and held the town of Myitkyina.

My research continued concentrating on any history about the 2nd Galahad force and in particular, my cousin's unit Company F. Undoubtedly, 2nd Galahad turned the tide at Myitkyina but received little credit for it. 2nd Galahad did not have the benefit of being able to train for a few weeks at least, with veterans of the fighting in Burma to give them a heads up about what they were about to face. No matter how well a soldier is trained, when the first shots are fired everything changes. No soldier knows exactly how he will react when he is suddenly in direct close combat with resounding noise and mass confusion. He may hit the dirt and cover his head. Or, he may face the direction of the incoming enemy fire and shoot and reload his weapon as fast as his instinct and training demand.

The 2nd Galahad men were rushed right up to the front lines to face the enemy. The Japanese used many unconventional tactics to confuse our troops, tactics that the trainers back in the states knew nothing about but were well known by the veterans of 1st Galahad. Japanese soldiers put on the uniforms of the captured and dead Chinese troops and waved at our GIs, encouraging them to move forward. When our men came close enough they were cut down by cross fire from Japanese machine guns that were "zeroed in" and aiming directly at our troops' positions. Too few original experienced Marauders were around to warn 2nd Galahad about these tactics.

At the 'Siege of Myitkyina," of the original 2,500 2nd Galahad and the remaining few hundred 1st Galahad, 272 were killed in action, 955 wounded, and 980 evacuated for sickness, some later dying. Heavy losses were also sustained by the Chinese with 972 killed in action, 3,184 wounded and 168 for sickness. As is true in all battles, many mistakes were made on both sides.

Perhaps greater coordination between Stilwell and the area air commander to guide our attack planes would have reduced allied casualties. However, here again Stilwell and the army air corps had long standing feuds over tactics dealing with the infantry soldier versus air power. My reading about Stilwell tells me that he was not totally in favor of combined air and ground force tactics in the combat environment of Burma and China. I do not recall reading a single comment about Stilwell inviting Air Corp personnel on the ground with his troops to direct and coordinate air support so common in all combat areas and, I might add, very, very welcomed by the troops on the ground.

It seems Stilwell fought not only the Japanese, but he also fought with the British, referring to them as "Limeys. He tactlessly referred to Chiang Kei Shek as "Peanut" (behind his back, of course) not realizing and too naïve to know Chiang had secret ears all around Stilwell. In Gavin Mortimer's "Merrill's Marauders" on page 188, a 1st Galahad soldier was quoted as saying after Stilwell visited the front lines, "I had him in my sights and could have killed the bastard. No one would know the difference and would just have blamed it on a Jap sniper." Almost all the area's top commanders, both American and Allies as well, requested President Roosevelt to remove Stilwell from the CBI Theater.

Almost the entire Japanese force of 4,600 were killed defending the town, and only 187 enemy troops were captured. The Japanese commanders were ordered to fight to the last man to hold the town and regain the air base. One Japanese commander was known to have committed suicide when Myitkyina fell. Another was ordered by Tokyo to shoot himself, which he did because, he had failed and disappointed the Emperor. The Japanese second in command was allowed by his superiors to escape across the Irrawaddy River with several hundred soldiers only to be hunted down and killed by Detachment 101 OSS-led Kachin guerilla forces.

Myitkyina was the important battle that helped to drive the Japanese out of Northern Burma. The fighting in Burma continued until the war's end, and the CBI Theater finally got a bigger share of our massive assets. But American men were still fighting and dying in the mountains, parched plains and jungles of Burma.

Ironically, the sick and wounded GIs evacuated from Myitkyina were all issued jungle hammocks with protective sand fly netting and rain covers that were denied the Marauders at the beginning of the operation. Had Stilwell's G-4 supply officer dug deeper to find these hammocks and issued them to 1st Galahad, much of the terrible diseases that dissipated the men would undoubtedly have been prevented. This was only one of the many details Stilwell's people overlooked. It's a wonder Stilwell himself didn't think about this.

Earlier in the war, in 1942, the Japanese forces overwhelmed the Allies. Stilwell led several hundred American and allied troops on a forced march on foot, through the Burmese jungles and then over the mountains into India. He proved to be a strong leader in that retreat operation and later commented, “I claim we got a hell of a beating. We got run out of Burma, and it was humiliating as hell. I think we should find out what caused it and go back and take it.” Old “Vinegar Joe“ should have checked the details or at least, as many great combat leaders have done, assigned a detail man to work with the staff to assure the mission was well planned and the troops were well armed, well equipped, well informed, and well fed.

When assembling for the final battle at Myitkyina, there were only about 300 men of the original 2,750 men of the 1st Galahad Force that were still fit for duty. They desperately needed replacements if they were to take the town of Myitkyina or for that matter to even hold the recently captured air base. It is for this reason that 2nd Galahad was formed and so urgently needed.

The 5307th was a regimental-sized unit but never had their own colors (flag) nor did they have their own unique regimental crest (insignia) as all other regimental-sized units had. No official shoulder patch or recognition was ever authorized for the Marauders during their operations.

Later on in August 1944, the unit was unceremoniously disbanded and the many promised promotions and decorations were just ignored or forgotten. Many of the officers who recommended these awards and promotions to their deserving Marauders, were either killed or died of disease or wounds in the area's several hospitals located in Burma and also in better equipped hospitals in India.

The tattered remnants of the original 1st Galahad 2750 volunteers of the 5307th were treated very badly by those at headquarters. These men were combined with the 475th Infantry Regiment and continued the fight in Burma as the "Mars Task Force." All the promises from Stilwell and his staff for a break to rest and nourish themselves were all forgotten and ignored.

Many years later and long after my cousin was killed, the memories of those times were filed away in the deep recesses of my memory. That history book I picked up in the library alerted me to the fact that Vincent served with the Merrill's Marauders. What bothered me most was that Vincent's parents, his brother, and the Cavallo family knew nothing at all about his service and his wartime experience. I realized I had a lot of work to do and continued reading everything I could about the 5307th.

I remembered writing him that one V-mail letter using the odd-sounding address which was never answered because, he had been already killed by the time the letter arrived in Burma. The V-mail was the government's effort to make uniform the mail overseas to speed up the delivery time. And it may have even been a little less postage. I believe military personnel serving overseas could send letters postage free, and it seemed everyone at home used V-mail.

A lifetime later in 1995 I registered at the VA to have my hearing tested and asked the attendant to check my cousin's record. She brought his scant service record right up on the screen with his serial number, date of death, 28 Jun 1944, Purple Heart medal, Asiatic Pacific service medal with one bronze campaign star, and the World War Two Victory Medal. There was some cursory mention of his training at Camp Swift, Texas, and that was all. This encouraged me and sparked my interest and I became further energized after reading that library book. Now, with Vincent's name, rank, and proper serial number, I took advantage of the Freedom of Information Act.

I wrote letters to multiples of army sources requesting copies of his complete records. I went a step further and paid a fee to the U.S. Army Historical Institute and received a thick envelope with documents about Vincent's service in the 5307th. My continuing research included writing to the U.S. Navy to find the name of the troopship that carried him to Asia. Also, the dates and times and all the ports the troopship visited before the final destination in India. I read some interesting facts about the voyage and the description of the ship as well.

I contacted my first cousin Jackie Cavalla, my Aunt Lucy's daughter who is the Cavallo family historian. To this very day, she posts on Facebook.com old family photos most of us have never seen before of our Cavallo family. The pictures were taken by her mother years ago in the 1930's and 1940's.

Jackie directed me to Vincent's nephew and namesake who never knew his uncle. His father was Vincent's brother Raymond who, remained close to his parents in the Bronx. Unfortunately, Raymond passed away years before my research began. I received some photos from Vincent's nephew who, was a great help to me in filling in many missing anecdotal details to complete my narrative about his uncle's service. As a child he recalled hearing talk about his uncle from his father and his grandfather. They recalled hearsay stories told to them by some of Private Cavallo's comrades who visited them in the Bronx after the war.

These stories told to Vincent's parent's were some interesting comments about having "volunteered with Vincent for more dangerous duty." I was now left with an interesting clue about the reason my cousin Vincent was in the 5307th in the first place.

Did he volunteer? His buddies told his parents they volunteered with Vincent. This made me take a closer look at the actual furlough orders in Vincent's records. I thought it odd to see two separate orders. One reading a ten day furlough showing starting dates and ending dates. The second order showed the same for the additional five days. Why did the army use two separate orders and not simply have one order showing a fifteen day furlough?

Was it by chance…or did he volunteer? Was this the reason Vincent received the extra five days before he left for overseas duty to someplace unknown to him at the time?

This question remained in my mind for a long time. Did Vincent volunteer with his buddies? Was that the reason he received a generous furlough as a reward for volunteering for a more dangerous duty and, did he pay for it with his life. We wonder if the entire complement of the 2,500 men in Vincent's group all volunteered. I doubt that because if it was true then a simple order for a fifteen-day furlough would have been written for everyone.

Soldiers were promised an incentive to volunteer and one of the rewards was for some extra furlough time to spend with their family and friends. Some couples even took advantage of the added days to get married and spend this precious time together. Only God knows how many babies were created so that brides would have some part of their cherished one if he never returned. The one leaving might also feel he would leave a part of himself should he fall in battle never to see his loved ones again.

Only those who experienced these feelings of love and longing would understand sharing these same thoughts. At times of war sweethearts throughout the world have made these same decisions to confirm their vows of love to each other.

Chapter 7

Vincent Comes Home

My Uncle Fred Cavallo I was to learn much later in my life, was actually christened Ottavio. He probably chose Freddie for the same reason my Mom Donatella picked Nellie because to them, it sounded more American. My mom was only one year old when she arrived here from Italy with her parents and older brother Joseph. Fred was to remain in Italy by the demand of my Grandfathers mother. The reason for this family mystery is still unfolding. The Cavallo's were from a village high in the mountains of Campagna, in the Provence of Salerno, Italy. Home to both the Cavallo's and Chiara's my grandmother's family.

I received copies of all of Vincent's army records including, copies of some very personal documents. Among the records I received were copies of letters written by my Uncle Fred Cavallo to the Commanding Officers first of the 5307th, and when it was disbanded, to the Commanding Officer of the 475th Infantry Regiment. His letters were all appeals to the army to return his son's remains home for burial. The hiatus from 5307th to 475th caused further disruptions in the continuity of not only my cousin's army records but, hundreds more of his fellow soldiers who had served in the 5307th.

The records I received revealed Vincent was first buried next to his comrades in a U.S. military cemetery in Myitkyina, Burma, close to where he had fallen in 1944. In January 1945, his remains were moved to a U.S. military cemetery in Kalaikunda, India. After two more years of correspondence between Vincent's parents and the U.S. Army, he was finally returned home in December, 1946. A soldier escorted Vincent's flag-draped coffin to Edward Piacente Funeral Home at 285 East 149th Street in the Bronx. He is buried now in Saint Raymond's Cemetery in the Bronx. I was 14 years old and I remember the wake and funeral. It was very, very sad. Vincent was finally home from the war.

At the wake I overheard talk from my uncles about the identity of the remains in the coffin. I researched the long journey Vincent's remains took to arrive home and, I am certain and confident that Vincent was returned to his parents for burial at home as his family wished.

While reviewing all the records, I was very impressed with the care and precision with which the Army Graves Registration soldiers carried out their duty to accurately identify the fallen. One of the two metal ID dog tags remain forever with the individual soldier's remains. The burial site numbers are retained to keep an accurate record of these burial locations of the individual soldier and his grave site. This insured that an accurate record followed the remains, showing the exact locations and plot numbers as each soldier was interred and then reburied. This further assured continuity of identity. This of course, was before anyone knew anything at all about DNA to prove relationship.

All the very personal records I received were forwarded to Private Cavallo's nephew, who was the closest and only remaining next of kin. The soldier's life is quickly lost, but the family mourns for a lifetime.

In 1980 when my dad, John Gallagher, passed away, Uncle Louie Cavallo with whom I had no contact since the 1950s, came to the wake. My uncle also served in World War II as a rifleman in France. He mentioned to me that he met a veteran who was with Vincent when he was killed. At that time I was under great business pressures and did not follow up with a phone call to my Uncle Louie. Unfortunately, my uncle passed away long before my research began, and I never had the opportunity to talk to him about Vincent.

The facts about Vincent's service greatly interested me as I looked for answers and I read profusely about the China Burma India Theater and the 5307th. Early in my research, I thought Vincent may have been with the original 1st Galahad volunteers. I even found on online a roster of all the 3,000 names of the original 1st Galahad Force. The name of Private Rocky Cavallo a medic, appeared on the list and for a while, I thought this might be Vincent. I could even see him with a nickname of "Rocky." Or, it may just have been wishful thinking until, I obtained more detailed records and checked serial numbers and dates only to find this could not be Vincent.

July 1944 the army awarded the 5307th with a Distinguished Unit Citation, which was an award given to combat units for exemplary performance. Later, in 1966 the award was recognized by the president of the United States and elevated to the Presidential Unit Citation.

At some later date the Department of the Army finally honored the 5307th with a rare distinction; it awarded every member serving with the unit in Burma, the Bronze Star Medal. This was for the length of time the unit was in constant combat with the enemy. The rear echelon of a few 5307th members remained in India and never went to Burma and were denied the medal. A further award originating in World War II exclusively for the combat infantrymen, was the revered "Combat Infantry Badge," still awarded and proudly worn by many infantry soldiers today.

The battle of Myitkyina was so chaotic with fatal errors on both sides that no time was made to sort out the details. The wounded were evacuated to field hospitals in Burma by air, and the dead buried at the site of the battle. Nothing appeared on Vincent's record that he was in the 5307th and there is no mention of the other decorations he earned at such great cost to his young life. I felt it was my duty to correct these omissions on my cousin's record.

I compiled a chronological paper trail of Private Cavallo's records showing Vincent's complete service from his induction as a draftee at Camp Upton to his death at Myitkyina while serving with the 5307th.

This was sent to my then Pennsylvania U.S. Senator, Arlen Specter. I asked for his help to have the army update my cousin's service record. Once verified by the army, it resulted in their approval to make corrections to Vincent's army personnel record.

On a follow up phone call to Senator Specter's office in Philadelphia I spoke to his aide, Mr. Verne Rider. He told me he was also stationed at Camp Swift, Texas, many years after my cousin. Vern assured me he would personally follow up for speedy action to honor my request.

After serving his country my cousin Vincent, would have enjoyed the blessing of returning home to his family but, this was not to be realized for him. Instead of a happy home coming party his mom and dad and brother spent a lifetime of sorrow over the loss of their beloved son and brother.

Vincent was among the 407,000 fallen heroes from World War II. The joy and blessing of returning home was just not to be theirs. We want to remember Vincent and honor him along with all the brave men and women who made the supreme sacrifice while serving our nation in all our wars, past and present.

I cannot help but reflect upon my own homecoming when sailing under the Golden Gate Bridge in San Francisco and joining in with the shout of joy of 4,000 soldiers happy to arrive home safely from the Korean War. That outburst must have resounded from the Coit Tower to Mount Tamalpias.

Many fallen heroes' stories were never told and it is for this reason, I wanted to tell my cousin's story for him. Any veteran who has served knows the real heroes are those who bear the wounds and the physical and mental scars and above all, those who never came back. Those heroes who never again saw the smiles of joy and relief on the faces of their loved ones. They would never again feel the warm embraces from their family nor the affectionate kisses from their sweethearts.

We pray that Vincent rests in peace in the presence of our Lord and we ask the Lord's Blessings for you, Private Vincent Cavallo, Serial Number 32 XXX XXX, F Company 5307th Composite Unit, Provisional, 2nd Galahad Force, "Merrill's Marauders."

We want everyone to know who you were and what you did for your country.

Your cousin,
Vincent G. Gallagher
2019

Illustrations

Brigadier General Frank D. Merrill
and
Lieutenant General Joseph W. Stilwell,
Burma, 1944

US Military Photo (Public Domain)
via Wikipedia Commons

Illustrations

British Major General
Orde Charles Wingate
Burma, 1943

US Military Photo
(Public Domain via Wikipedia Commons)

Illustrations

Lieutenant General Joseph W. Stilwell
and British Lord Louis Mountbatten
Supreme Area Commander of all Allied
Forces in the China, Burma, India Theater.

(Public Domain) via Wikipedia Commons)

Illustrations

Private Vincent Cavallo
wearing the 97th Infantry Division
shoulder patch. Taken at
Fort Leonard Wood, Missouri
prior to his final furlough.

With Mom on the furlough from
Camp Swift, Texas July 1943

Vincent and his mom taken in the Bronx, showing the happy smiles I remembered as a child of my cousin, Vincent, and my Aunt Mary Cavallo.

Illustrations

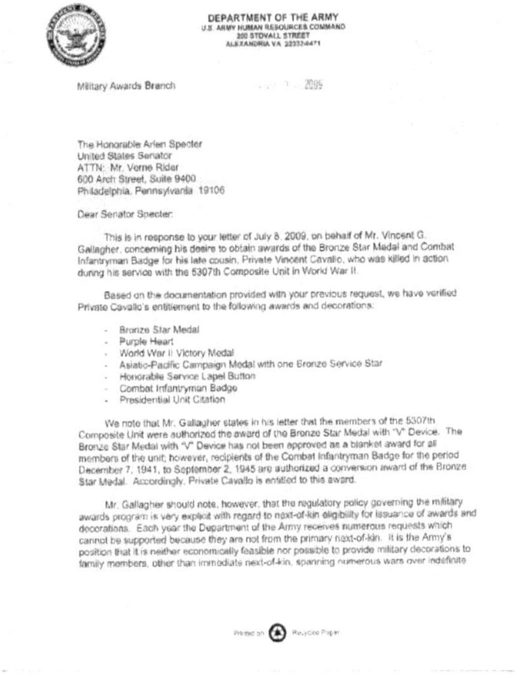

DEPARTMENT OF THE ARMY
U.S. ARMY HUMAN RESOURCES COMMAND
200 STOVALL STREET
ALEXANDRIA VA 22332-0471

Military Awards Branch

The Honorable Arlen Specter
United States Senator
ATTN: Mr. Verne Rider
600 Arch Street, Suite 9400
Philadelphia, Pennsylvania 19106

Dear Senator Specter:

This is in response to your letter of July 8, 2009, on behalf of Mr. Vincent G. Gallagher, concerning his desire to obtain awards of the Bronze Star Medal and Combat Infantryman Badge for his late cousin, Private Vincent Cavallo, who was killed in action during his service with the 5307th Composite Unit in World War II.

Based on the documentation provided with your previous request, we have verified Private Cavallo's entitlement to the following awards and decorations:

- Bronze Star Medal
- Purple Heart
- World War II Victory Medal
- Asiatic-Pacific Campaign Medal with one Bronze Service Star
- Honorable Service Lapel Button
- Combat Infantryman Badge
- Presidential Unit Citation

We note that Mr. Gallagher states in his letter that the members of the 5307th Composite Unit were authorized the award of the Bronze Star Medal with "V" Device. The Bronze Star Medal with "V" Device has not been approved as a blanket award for all members of the unit; however, recipients of the Combat Infantryman Badge for the period December 7, 1941, to September 2, 1945 are authorized a conversion award of the Bronze Star Medal. Accordingly, Private Cavallo is entitled to this award.

Mr. Gallagher should note, however, that the regulatory policy governing the military awards program is very explicit with regard to next-of-kin eligibility for issuance of awards and decorations. Each year the Department of the Army receives numerous requests which cannot be supported because they are not from the primary next-of-kin. It is the Army's position that it is neither economically feasible nor possible to provide military decorations to family members, other than immediate next-of-kin, spanning numerous wars over indefinite

Printed on Recycled Paper

Department of the Army letter
August 2009, page 1

Illustrations

-2-

periods of time. Posthumous awards can only be issued to primary next-of-kin starting with the spouse, eldest child, father or mother, eldest brother or sister, or eldest grandchild. Regrettably, as Private Cavallo's cousin, this office is unable to provide the decorations to Mr. Gallagher.

Although the Department of the Army cannot issue these awards, they are available for purchase from private vendors who offer military memorabilia for sale to the public. We are enclosing a listing of certified manufacturers of these military decorations should Mr. Gallagher desire to purchase them.

We have also enclosed permanent orders authorizing the award of the Purple Heart, Bronze Star Medal, Combat Infantryman Badge and Presidential Unit Citation, as well as the Purple Heart certificate and Bronze Star Medal certificate. We have also forwarded this information to the National Personnel Records Center for inclusion in Private Cavallo's Official Military Personnel File.

We note that Mr. Gallagher has conducted extensive research regarding his late cousin's military service during World War II. If he has not already done so, he may wish to contact the National Archives at College Park, 8601 Adelphi Road, College Park, Maryland 20740-6001. The records archived with this agency may contain additional historical documents that make mention of Private Cavallo's service with the 5307th Composite Unit. When writing to the National Archives, Mr. Gallagher should include his cousin's dates of service, unit of assignment and service number. This information will allow them to conduct a thorough search of available records.

It is an honor to verify these symbols in recognition of Private Cavallo's faithful and dedicated service to our Nation during a time of great need. We appreciate your support of our Veterans, and the men and women serving in America's Army today.

Sincerely,

Stephen H. Harmon III
Lieutenant Colonel, U.S. Army
Acting Chief, Military Awards Branch

Enclosures

Department of the Army letter
August 2009, page 2

Illustrations

DEPARTMENT OF THE ARMY
U.S. ARMY HUMAN RESOURCES COMMAND
200 STOVALL STREET
ALEXANDRIA, VA 22332-0471

PERMANENT ORDER 078-24

19 March 2009

CAVALLO, VINCENT 32811789 PVT Company F, 5307th Composite Unit, Asiatic-Pacific Theater of Operations

Announcement is made of the following award

Award: Bronze Star Medal (Posthumous)
Date(s) or period of service: 28 June 1944
Authority: AR 600-8-22, Paragraph 3-14d(2)
Reason: For meritorious achievement in active ground combat.
Format: 320

This Permanent Order supersedes any previously issued order that may have been published announcing this award

BY ORDER OF THE SECRETARY OF THE ARMY:

MARION A. SALTERS
LTC, AR
Chief, Military Awards Branch

DISTRIBUTION:
USA HRC (AHRC-PDP-A) (1)
NPRC (1)
Next of Kin (2)

Bronze Star Award Order

Illustrations

THE UNITED STATES OF AMERICA

TO ALL WHO SHALL SEE THESE PRESENTS, GREETING: THIS IS TO CERTIFY THAT THE PRESIDENT OF THE UNITED STATES OF AMERICA AUTHORIZED BY EXECUTIVE ORDER, 24 AUGUST 1962 HAS AWARDED

THE BRONZE STAR MEDAL

TO PRIVATE VINCENT CAVALLO
ARMY OF THE UNITED STATES

FOR meritorious achievement while serving with Company F, 5307th Composite Unit, in the Asiatic-Pacific Theater of Operations on 28 June 1944, in military operations against an armed enemy of the United States during World War II. Private Cavallo's exemplary performance of duty in active ground combat was in keeping with the finest traditions of military service and reflects great credit upon himself, the 5307th Composite Unit, and the Army of the United States.

GIVEN UNDER MY HAND IN THE CITY OF WASHINGTON
THIS 19TH DAY OF MARCH 2009

Bronze Star Award Medal

Illustrations

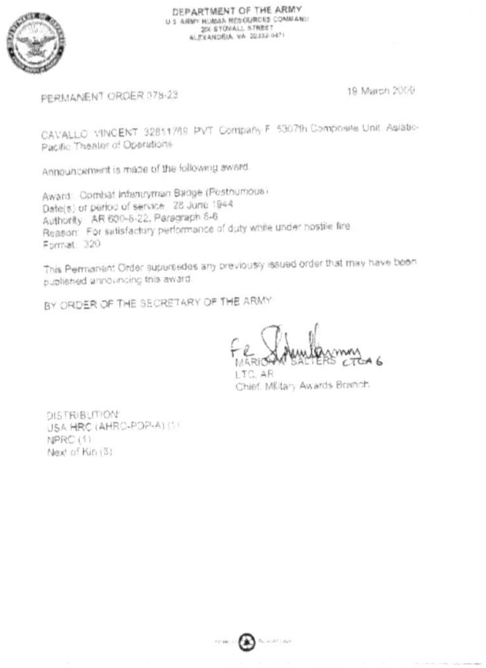

DEPARTMENT OF THE ARMY
U.S. ARMY HUMAN RESOURCES COMMAND
200 STOVALL STREET
ALEXANDRIA, VA 22332-0471

PERMANENT ORDER 078-23 19 March 2009

CAVALLO, VINCENT, 32811769, PVT, Company F, 5307th Composite Unit, Asiatic-Pacific Theater of Operations

Announcement is made of the following award.

Award: Combat Infantryman Badge (Posthumous)
Date(s) of period of service: 28 June 1944
Authority: AR 600-8-22, Paragraph 8-6
Reason: For satisfactory performance of duty while under hostile fire
Format: 320

This Permanent Order supersedes any previously issued order that may have been published announcing this award.

BY ORDER OF THE SECRETARY OF THE ARMY:

MARION A. SALTERS
LTC, AR
Chief, Military Awards Branch

DISTRIBUTION:
USA HRC (AHRC-PDP-A) (1)
NPRC (1)
Next of Kin (3)

Combat Infantryman Badge

Illustrations

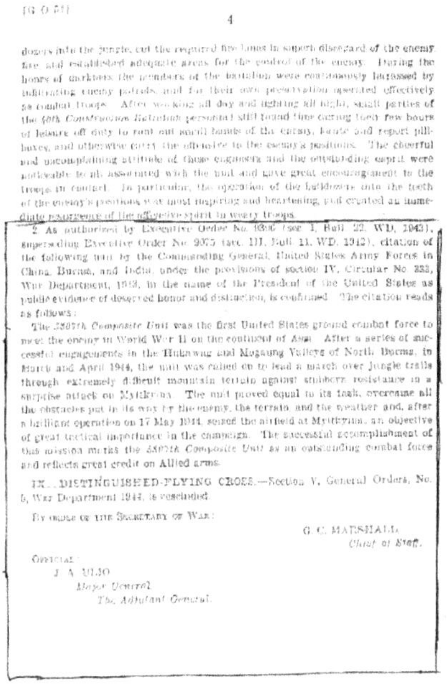

[G O 51]

4

dozers into the jungle, cut the required fire lanes in superb disregard of the enemy fire and established adequate areas for the control of the enemy. During the hours of darkness the members of the battalion were continuously harassed by infiltrating enemy patrols and for their own preservation operated effectively as combat troops. After working all day and fighting all night, small parties of the *60th Construction Battalion* personnel still found time during their few hours of leisure off duty to rout out small bands of the enemy, locate and report pillboxes, and otherwise carry the offensive to the enemy's positions. The cheerful and uncomplaining attitude of these engineers and the outstanding esprit were noticeable to all associated with the unit and gave great encouragement to the troops in contact. In particular, the operation of the bulldozers into the teeth of the enemy's positions was most inspiring and heartening, and created an immediate resurgence of the offensive spirit in weary troops.

2. As authorized by Executive Order No. 9396 (sec. I, Bull. 22, WD, 1943), superseding Executive Order No. 9075 (sec. III, Bull. 11, WD, 1942), citation of the following unit by the Commanding General, United States Army Forces in China, Burma, and India, under the provisions of section IV, Circular No. 333, War Department, 1943, in the name of the President of the United States as public evidence of deserved honor and distinction, is confirmed. The citation reads as follows:

The *5307th Composite Unit* was the first United States ground combat force to meet the enemy in World War II on the continent of Asia. After a series of successful engagements in the Hukawng and Mogaung Valleys of North Burma, in March and April 1944, the unit was called on to lead a march over jungle trails through extremely difficult mountain terrain against stubborn resistance in a surprise attack on Myitkyina. The unit proved equal to its task, overcame all the obstacles put in its way by the enemy, the terrain, and the weather and, after a brilliant operation on 17 May 1944, seized the airfield at Myitkyina, an objective of great tactical importance in the campaign. The successful accomplishment of this mission marks the *5307th Composite Unit* as an outstanding combat force and reflects great credit on Allied arms.

IX.. DISTINGUISHED-FLYING CROSS.—Section V, General Orders, No. 5, War Department 1944, is rescinded.

BY ORDER OF THE SECRETARY OF WAR:

G. C. MARSHALL,
Chief of Staff.

OFFICIAL:
J. A. ULIO
Major General,
The Adjutant General.

Presidential Unit Citation

Illustrations

INFORMATION RELEASABLE UNDER THE FREEDOM OF INFORMATION ACT

Name
Cavallo, Vincent
Branch of Service and Serial/Service Number(s)
Army of the United States-32 811 769
Dates of Service
27 February 1943 to 28 June 1944

Duty Status
Death
Rank/Grade
Private
Salary
N/A
Source of Commission
N/A
Promotion Sequence Number
N/A
Assignments and Geographical Locations
Co A 303 Inf-Camp Swift, TX

Military Education
N/A

Decorations and Awards
WW II Victory Medal, Service Lapel Button WW II, Purple Heart Medal, Asiatic Pacific Theatre Campaign Medal w/1 Bronze Service Star, Service Lapel Button WW II

Transcript of Court-Martial Trial
Not in file
Photograph
N/A
Place of Entry
Bronx, NY
Place of Separation

FOR DECEASED VETERAN ONLY

Place of Birth
N/A
Date of Death
28 June 1944
Location of Death
Pacific Area
Place of Burial
N/A

NOTE: N/A denotes information is not available in the veteran's records

NATIONAL ARCHIVES AND RECORDS ADMINISTRATION NA FORM 13164 (Rev. 02-02)

Original NA Form 13164

Illustrations

INFORMATION RELEASABLE UNDER THE FREEDOM OF INFORMATION ACT

NAME:
Cavallo, Vincent

BRANCH OF SERVICE AND SERIAL/SERVICE NUMBER(S):
Army of the United States

DATES OF SERVICE:
February 27, 1943 to June 28, 1944

DUTY STATUS:
Death

RANK/GRADE:
Private

SALARY:
Not Available

SOURCE OF COMMISSION:
Not Available

PROMOTION SEQUENCE NUMBER:
Not Available

ASSIGNMENTS AND GEOGRAPHICAL LOCATIONS:
Company A, 303rd Infantry Regiment @ Camp Swift, Texas;
5307th Composite Unit

MILITARY EDUCATION:
Not Available

DECORATIONS AND AWARDS:
Asiatic-Pacific Campaign Medal with 1 bronze service star, Bronze Star Medal, Combat Infantryman Badge, Honorable Lapel Button, Presidential Unit Citation, Purple Heart Medal, and World War II Victory Medal

TRANSCRIPT OF COURT-MARTIAL TRIAL:
Not Available

PHOTOGRAPH:
Not Available

PLACE OF ENTRY:
Bronx, New York

PLACE OF SEPARATION:
Pacific Area

FOR DECEASED VETERAN ONLY

PLACE OF BIRTH
Not Available

DATE OF DEATH
June 28, 1944

LOCATION OF DEATH
Pacific Area

PLACE OF BURIAL
Not Available

NOTE: N/A denotes information is not available in the veteran's records

NATIONAL ARCHIVES AND RECORDS ADMINISTRATION NA FORM 13164 (Rev. 02-02)

Revised NA Form 13164

Illustrations

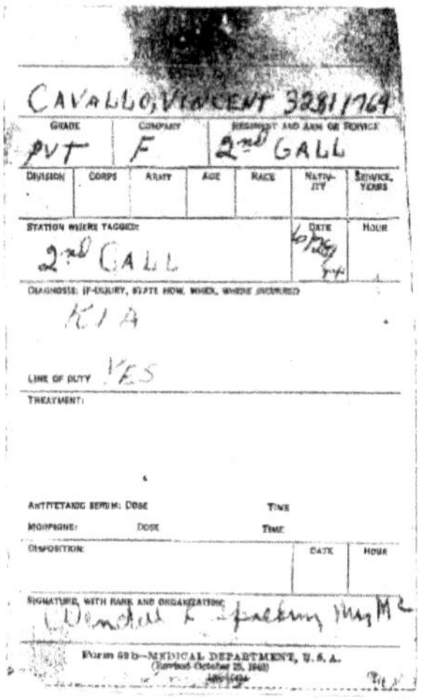

CAVALLO, VINCENT 32811764

GRADE: PVT
COMPANY: F
REGIMENT AND ARM OR SERVICE: 2nd GALL

DIVISION | CORPS | ARMY | AGE | RACE | NATIVITY | SERVICE, YEARS

STATION WHERE TAGGED: 2nd GALL
DATE: 6/26/44
HOUR

DIAGNOSIS: IF INJURY, STATE HOW, WHEN, WHERE INCURRED
KIA

LINE OF DUTY YES

TREATMENT:

ANTITETANIC SERUM: DOSE TIME
MORPHINE: DOSE TIME

DISPOSITION: DATE HOUR

SIGNATURE, WITH RANK AND ORGANIZATION:

Form 52b—MEDICAL DEPARTMENT, U. S. A.

US Army Medical Form 52B

Illustrations

Private Vincent Cavallo's
Medals and Awards

Acknowledgements

Very special thanks to my Aunt Lucy's daughter my first cousin, Jackie Cavalla who is the Cavallo family historian. Jackie has firsthand knowledge and maintained records and anecdotes about the family told to her by her mother. Jackie also remembers her young life growing up in close contact with her cousins and her grandparents Vincenzo and Maria Cavallo. Jackie's Mom, Lucille, took volumes of family photographs all during the 1930s and 1940s. Jackie has been kind enough to post these numerous historic family photos on Facebook.com for all the family to cherish.

Jackie also gave me the list of addresses of the entire Cavallo extended family. I sent them all a copy of the first 15-page narrative I wrote about Cousin Vincent back in 2009. Most never knew Vincent, and those in our family who did remember him did not know of his service with the Merrill's Marauders in Burma.

I am very thankful to have renewed my contact with my Grandmother Maria's Chiara side of my family through Mary Bosch. My mother and Mary's mother were first cousins and very close as I remember them as a child. We all lived close together with the Cavallo's in Woodside and the Chiara's lived in Astoria both, in Queens County, New York City.

Acknowledgements

Mary Bosch's grandfather, Michael Chiara, was my Great Uncle Mike. Mary is quite knowledgeable and is also a historian having documented both the Cavallo and the Chiara family's histories. Both families are from Colliano, the same small mountain village in the Province of Salerno, Italy. Her knowledge was obtained directly from word of mouth and observation from the closeness of growing up with all her mother's family living nearby in Queens County.

Mary's grandfather was Great Uncle Mike to scores of nieces and nephews and he graced the Chiara and Cavallo families for 106 years. At his 100th birthday party celebration filmed in full color, he appeared to be in excellent health and spirits. He is seen as he was interviewed by his grandchildren including Mary, when they asked him questions about the details of his long personal history. He stood before the camera straight, trim, and articulate with his colorful Italian accent exactly as I remembered him. Except now, his hair was white and he wore black horn-rimmed glasses which, I never saw him wear when he read the Italian newspapers. He delivered an unbroken review of his life, recalling the times and the events and is remembered by all, to be an inspiration for his positive attitude and awareness.

My cousin, Mary Bosch, contributed to the precious history of the Chiara and Cavallo origins in Colliano. She was fortunate to have visited the small village of Colliano with her mother, Carmela Chiara Celauro, known by all as "Millie." The village appeared to still look charming with old world beauty and modern 21st Century conveniences. And, the Cavallo and Chiara descendant's all looked healthy and prosperous.

Millie appeared in the film when she was an octogenarian and briskly climbing steps carved out of the steep rock outcropping to visit an old and historic Catholic chapel high on the mountain top in Colliano.

When my wife Lee and I visited Mary and Charlie Bosch's home, we viewed the wonderful color movies taken by Mary and her brother when they were in Colliano where, some of my own roots are planted. I would have easily recognized the faces of the Cavallo's and Chiara's I saw in those movies for their very familiar facial qualities and predominant blue eyes. That encounter was an education for me about my own family's rich history that I never heard about growing up in

Woodside. It was indeed an enlightening and emotional experience for me.

When at the Bosch's home on that visit I talked to Mary's mother. She was 96 years old and sitting there doing word puzzles at the time and...looked great! Millie did not recognize me for I had not seen her since I was a young boy. But, as soon as Mary mentioned my Mother Nellie Gallagher, she remembered. Thank you, Mary and Charlie Bosch, for that warm, heartfelt experience. That was a special day for me and my wife Lee.

Thank you to Private Cavallo's nephew and namesake, Vincent Cavallo, who never knew his uncle, only the anecdotes he heard from his father, Raymond, and grandparents, Fred and Mary Cavallo. Vincent helped me put many of the missing pieces together and sent me pictures of his grandmother Mary and his Uncle Vincent on that final furlough. Thanks to my brother, Jim Gallagher and my Sister-in-Law Kay, who kept the picture of Vincent that was on display for years in our parents' home.

Thank you again Rosemary Augustine for making my second book with you a reality. You have shared so much of your publishing talents to take a rough narrative and help make it a book. Blessings to you from both me and my wife, Lee.

Acknowledgements

Thanks also to, Katherine McKay, who lent her editing skills in putting commas in the right places and sentences in the proper order.

My grateful thanks and thoughts go to those multitudes of brave men and women in uniform today who volunteer to serve. They raise their right hand and step forward dedicating their lives to protect every one of us blessed to be an American.

Bibliography

Collections Consulted

U.S. Army National Archives and Record Administration.

U.S. Army, Deceased Personnel file.

Entry # 315 National War College by Col. Charles Newton Hunter. 3 Aug. 1944 downgraded to Secret.

U.S. Army Heritage and Education Center.

U.S. Army Military History Institute.

U.S. Army Human Resource Command Individual.

U.S. Army Medical Department Book 5. 5307th The Marauders and the Microbes.

97th Infantry Division History.

The Marauders Association.

Wikipedia, Merrill's Marauders.

CIA: Aspects of Intelligence Galahad

Bibliography

U.S. Army Troop Transports World War II

U.S. Navy Troopships World War II

Military Sea Transportation Service
Troopships World War II

Phone interview with veteran of 1st Galahad

Books

Walk Out with Stilwell in Burma, Frank Dorn

Stilwell, D.D. Rooney.

Stilwell and the American Experience in China, Barbara W. Tuchman.

The Last Empress Madame Chiang Kei Shek, Hanna Pakula.

Chiang Kei Shek's Teacher and Ambassador, Mei Le Tong

The Marauders, LT/Colonel Charlton Ogburn.

Bibliography

Merrill's Marauders, Gavin Mortimer

Galahad, LT/Colonel Charles Newton Hunter.

Merrill's Marauders, Combined operations in Northern Burma in 1944, Dr. Gary J. Bjorge.

Burma Surgeon, Dr. Gordon S. Seagrave.

Flying Tiger: The True Story of General Claire Chennault and the 14th Air Force in China, James Samson

Flying Tiger Chennault in China, Robert Lee Scott, Jr.

The Maverick War: Chennault and the Flying Tigers, Duane P. Shultz,

The Flying Tigers, Sam Kleiner

Lord Mountbatten: The Last Viceroy, David Butler

Personal Diary of Admiral The Lord Louis Mountbatten Supreme Allied Commander Southeast Asia, 1943-1946, Earl and Philip Ziegler

Bibliography

In the 1940's the China Burma India Theater of Operation (CBI) was one of the most hazardous areas for American forces to serve. Just being in that threatening area and away from any immediate combat action, exposed the troops to deadly diseases. These microbes claimed the lives of thousands of allied and enemy forces as well as the local inhabitants.

CBI Shoulder Patch

Visit author website which includes additional books, pictures, and stories.
VinceGallagherBooks.com

. . .